THE
DEATH OF GOD
DEBATE

THE
DEATH OF GOD
DEBATE

THE
DEATH OF GOD
DEBATE

Edited by

JACKSON LEE ICE
and
JOHN J. CAREY

Philadelphia
THE WESTMINSTER PRESS

Copyright © MCMLXVII The Westminster Press

Scripture quotations from the Revised Standard Version
of the Bible are copyright, 1946 and 1952, by the Division of Christian Education of the National Council of
Churches, and are used by permission.

LIBRARY OF CONGRESS CATALOG CARD NO. 67-15088

Published by The Westminster Press ®
Philadelphia, Pennsylvania

PRINTED IN THE UNITED STATES OF AMERICA

PREFACE

T HE APPEARANCE of this book is the result not only of the interest of the editors but also of the support and encouragement of The Westminster Press and the friendly counsel of Professors William Hamilton and Thomas Altizer. Professors Hamilton and Altizer have given freely of their time in interviews with us, have offered valuable suggestions concerning the format of the book, and, amid busy schedules, have contributed new articles for this volume. We are also grateful to the various authors and publishers who have allowed us to reprint their work in this effort to clarify some of the issues raised by the "death of God" theologians.

We wish to acknowledge our thanks to Mrs. Anne Gandy, Mrs. Pamela Hamilton, and Miss Lana Paulk for their assistance in typing the manuscript, and to Mrs. Mary Charlotte Love for her capable handling of so many matters as she assisted us in the preparation of this book.

J. J. C.
J. L. I.

Tallahassee, Florida

CONTRIBUTORS

Jackson Lee Ice is Associate Professor of Religion and Philosophy at Florida State University, Tallahassee, Florida.

John L. Carey is Associate Professor of Religion and Dean of Students at Florida State University, Tallahassee, Florida.

Paul H. Wright is Assistant Professor of Psychology at the University of North Dakota, Grand Forks, North Dakota.

Fred M. Hudson is Chaplain and Assistant Professor of Religion at Colby College in Maine.

Warren L. Moulton is Associate Professor of Parish Ministry and Field Education at Central Baptist Theological Seminary, Kansas City, Kansas.

Theodore Runyon, Jr., is Associate Professor of Systematic Theology at the Candler School of Theology at Emory University, Atlanta, Georgia.

Harmon R. Holcomb is Professor of Theology at Colgate Rochester Theological School in Rochester, New York.

Julian Hartt is Noah Porter Professor of Philosophical Theology and Chairman of the Department of Religion at Yale University, New Haven, Connecticut.

F. Thomas Trotter is Dean and Associate Professor of Religion and the Arts at the Southern California School of Theology at Claremont.

Daniel Callahan is Associate Editor of *Commonweal*.

Arthur Hertzberg is Rabbi of Temple Emanu-El in Englewood, New Jersey.

James Alvin Sanders is Professor of Old Testament at Union Theological Seminary in New York.

Paul L. Holmer is Professor of Theology at Yale University.

Gabriel Vahanian is Associate Professor of Religion at Syracuse University.

W. M. Alexander is Associate Professor of Religion and Philosophy at St. Andrews College, Laurinburg, North Carolina.

William Hamilton is Professor of Theology at Colgate Rochester Divinity School.

Thomas J. J. Altizer is Associate Professor of Religion at Emory University.

CONTENTS

PART III

SELECTED CORRESPONDENCE: THE RESPONSE
OF THE PUBLIC AT LARGE

PART IV

THE FUTURE OF THE RADICAL THEOLOGY:
THE THEOLOGIANS SPEAK FOR THEMSELVES

Jackson Lee Ice and *John J. Carey*

INTRODUCTION

I

THE "death of God" controversy, which has rattled stained-glass windows throughout the whole country and piqued Americans into becoming amateur theologians overnight, is an unusual phenomenon for many reasons.

First of all, the whole thing apparently began as the result of a happy editorial accident. A staff writer for *The New Yorker* magazine, while writing a series on the English Bishop John A. T. Robinson and his provocative book *Honest to God,* inadvertently came upon the American radicals and decided to do an article on them. He had been working on it for almost a year when, just prior to its appearance on the newsstands, the religion writer for *The New York Times,* having read on his own an article by William Hamilton in the *Christian Scholar* (Spring, 1965), wrote a column entitled "'New' Theologians See Christianity Without God." This was on October 17, 1965. There then followed in rapid-fire succession articles in *The New Yorker, Time* magazine, and the *New York Herald Tribune.* These were apparently the first sparks that exploded the radical theology across the land. From then on, through widely syndicated columns and featured magazine articles, the affair was pumped and driven along by expanding publicity to the very top of the journalistic hit parade. The garbled event got out of hand with wilder and wilder reports and poorer and poorer rewrites by second-rate newspapers. As Hamilton noted, "the reaction overwhelmed the original event," and the whole thing became a "pseudo-event" in the public world "in which angry men were fighting non-existent enemies, and people were reacting to things never spoken." Meetings were called, letters written, telephone calls made, conferences planned, radio and TV appearances scheduled, sermons preached, and books contracted, until in a short time its exaggerated proportions gave it all the appearance of a theological Armageddon. Prematurely hurled into the glare of public opinion, the surprised theologians unexpectedly found themselves in the middle of a so-called movement they never planned and were regarded as spokesmen for a theology they had not yet completely formulated.

Secondly, at the time of its appearance the "death of God" movement was not a movement. This was a false impression circulated mainly by the press. When one looked more closely into the matter, one surprisingly discovered that there were only three or four theologians, each working independently of one another, who had produced among them only a few books and scattered articles on the subject! Its impact was certainly disproportionate to its size. But besides this, their writings exhibited a wide variety of interest and viewpoint in which there was found as much disagreement as agreement. Where was the tightly knit group and the unanimity of belief? There was none. And outside of the usual coterie of professional readers in the theological ghettos who knew about their ideas, there was no great following.

Even today there is some question as to whether it is a movement or not. This is probably purely academic. Our contention is that it may still be too early to judge. At least those ardent detractors who took it as a passing craze have had to refocus their opinions, since the signs now read otherwise. The responses in favor of such a new theological venture are unexpectedly strong, and if the piles of letters that Altizer and Hamilton received over the past year are any indication, the number of interested participants is increasing. "While radical theology . . . has not yet become a self-conscious 'movement,'" write Altizer and Hamilton, "it nevertheless has gained the interest and in part the commitment of a large number of Christians in America."[1]

After witnessing the meteoric rise of an Elvis Presley, and the establishment of an empire by a group of Beatles, one is no longer astonished at what the organs of mass media can perform in the way of popularizing a fad or creating a nonexistent movement. It is easy to think of "Christian atheism" in this light and dismiss it as a theological gimmick conjured up to gain notoriety by sheer shock appeal. The only thing is that some fads have a way of becoming disturbingly permanent. This time when the journalistic dust had settled, the "death of God" theologians were still standing—in fact, a little taller than before—and casting a larger shadow.

Though not a movement to begin with, and perhaps not one yet, it at least survived the deadly flare of faddish publicity and is a serious contender for becoming a new religion current within Protestantism today. We must conclude that it is here to stay, whether we like it or not. In the opinion of certain knowledgeable observers, the churches cannot avoid the pertinent theological questions that it raises, regardless of how disturbing they are, for it is an honest attempt—from within the church, not outside it—to meet an inevitable crisis of faith which confronts religion today.

Thirdly, the controversy is unusual because of the surprising impact it has had upon students, ministers, and theologians| We are not referring to those who lightly dismissed it as heretical nonsense, nor to those patrons who are eternally in accord with whatever is new, but to the many in the religious community who were sobered, critically intrigued, secretly delighted, and enthusiastically attracted by the radical ferment. Whether or not they fully understood or agreed, they were strangely drawn; and they entered the fray of new ideas with earnest concern.

It is doubtful whether at any time before, at least in this country, a theological ax of such sharp determination and candor has attempted to sever Christianity so completely from its roots, or its adherents been called upon to revise so thoroughly its practices and allegiances. As Altizer said, "We are now entering a period in which Christianity must confront the most radical challenge it has faced since its beginning."[2] Yet an amazing number were willing to try. It left them without a God they could lay their hands on, yet they felt, underneath the turmoil, a healthy hunger for a more realistic and meaningful understanding of God. It left them theologically speechless—literally—without an adequate religious language to make sense out of what they wanted to say, yet they were eager enough for a fresh idiom and believed enough in the importance of such an enterprise to wait and work for a symbol system suitable for men come of age. It left them without a church in which to worship, yet they were willing to engage the secular order to rethink their ideas of divine service. It smoked out those who were hiding comfortably behind an outmoded theology, and encountered them with a new burning bush which they realized could not be quenched by spouting Biblical proof texts or stamped out with fancy theological footwork. Was it a sign, or another brush fire? Many answered by removing their shoes.

Perhaps some had come to the hard conclusion that in an age such as ours nothing less than a do-or-die attitude was required if religion was to survive. Or perhaps some consciously believed, as Martin Marty quipped, that "any new heresy is better than any old orthodoxy." We do not know. But they saw in the "death of God" theologies more of an opportunity than a threat; and, if anything, were impressed with the intellectual sincerity, moral fervor, and evangelistic determination of the young theologians.

Many reasons can be given for the strong appeal that it has had. Among them, certainly, is the fact that a fresh point of view came at a time in history when neo-orthodoxy, and with it some parts of historical Christianity, had reached the end of the line, and our society was secular or ready enough acutely to be aware of the need for such a radical religious change.

Fourthly, the catchphrase "death of God," or "God is dead," which the "new" theology employs, is not new. From the heated reactions that it stirred up, one would get the impression that such a pronouncement had never been heard before on this planet, when in fact it is an idea that has been outspokenly declared by philosophers, poets, theologians, and novelists since the French Revolution. A progeny of the eighteenth century, it has had a long line of venerable ancestors. Its sudden reappearance in the theology of today is the fruit of a progressive "eclipse of God" that has been taking place since the turn of the century. It is part of a long growing history of modern man conscientiously wrestling with the God myth. In this sense, it is not new, as any student of the history of ideas or theology knows. This is why it was more a shock to the laity than to the clergy when Altizer and Hamilton described the "new shape" of contemporary theology in these terms.

Yet why has the idea upset so many and aroused, in numerous cases, those strong reactions which prevent full understanding or the unbiased determination to seek out what is actually being said? Certainly the average reader is aware that the realization that God's presence has been withdrawn or been lost sight of, or that God is hidden or eclipsed, has been a recurrent theme in theology, in sermons, and in religious literature since World War II. No one else has to advertise the fact that neither God nor the church has the appeal and power in our lives and in society that it once had. And agnosticism, atheism, and humanism have been around for centuries. Then why?

We believe there are two reasons: first, because it came from *within* the church, and proclaimed the message as an asset instead of a liability; and secondly, because of the new twist given to it—namely, by Altizer—which declares that a transcendent Being whom people once worshiped literally died at a certain time in history.

Of course, this is the meaning it has for only *one* of the four radical theologians (and possibly two, if we understand Hamilton correctly, even though he gives it his own personal variation). As we shall see, for Vahanian it has a cultural meaning: God has passed out of our existence and become a dead entity for us because we crowded him out of our consciousnesses in creating and worshiping idols of our own ethnic likenesses; and for van Buren, who abjures the phrase altogether as nonsensical, God language is dead and we have no factual way of determining anything about such an entity— hence, the term "God" very likely has never referred to anything actual.

One amusing thing about the phrase that launched a thousand press releases was that at the time it appeared, the loudest critics seemed to be the most certain they knew exactly what it meant. This was most strange, considering the fact that to Hamilton and Altizer it was "rhetorical" and "ambiguous." Thus, while the public was reacting to it, some persons pontificating as if they knew its precise meaning, Altizer and Hamilton were busy clarifying it for themselves and working to give their

ideas more positive substance. Lately, in fact, we have
been informed by Hamilton that he has discovered ten
different possible interpretations of the statement "God
is dead"—most of them familiar variations on the old
theme.[3]

Fifthly, it is most unusual for a "religious" movement
to be based on the tenets of godlessness and religionless-
ness. Yet this is what is being proposed. "Never before,"
writes Altizer, "has faith been called upon to negate all
religious meaning."[4] "Consequently the theologian must
exist outside of the church: he can neither proclaim the
Word, celebrate the sacraments, nor rejoice in the presence of the Holy Spirit."[5] "I am denying that religion is
necessary . . . ,"[6] says Hamilton. "I do not see how
preaching, worship, prayer, ordination, the sacraments
can be taken seriously by the radical theologians."[7] "My
Protestantism has no God, has no faith in God, and
affirms both the death of God and the death of all forms
of theism."[8] "Simple, literal theism is wrong and qualified
literal theism is meaningless," concludes van Buren.[9] And
Vahanian enigmatically states, "The history of religion is
the history of spiritual degeneration."[10] It seems as if the
"new" religion is a Godless, religionless religion.

What is one to make of a "Godless theology," a "Christ-
less Christ," a "Christian atheism," a "desacralized sacrament," and a piffled "epiphany"? Is it any wonder that
the reading and listening public is a little confused? How
can one keep one's cognitive footing in a linguistic terrain
of so many crumbling meanings and dialectical cre-
vasses? Just what are these men talking about?

The churches in America are no strangers to new and
radical ideas, particularly since World War II: Bultmann's demythologizing of the Bible, Tillich's existentialist theology of culture, Bonhoeffer's Christianity "come
of age," and, more recently, Cox's *The Secular City* and
Bishop Robinson's *Honest to God*. Though perhaps im-

perceptible to the layman, nurtured on the expedient
evasion of new ideas by timorous clerics, each indelibly
has left its mark, either by being absorbed, modified, or
rejected. But "honest to God" is one thing, "honest there
is not God" is another. To proffer new reforms within the
church is one thing, but to take the position that Christianity must now negate all religious thinking and exist
in the absence of God is another—especially since this is
claimed to be the "real" message of the gospel and the
"true" essence of Christianity! What could such a Christianity be? one ponders. Certainly it is a most unusual
trend in religion.

Finally, since the "death of God" controversy is
actually the *climax* of a series of theological emphases
and events that have occurred since the beginning of the
nineteenth century, it is not a totally new and foreign
intruder into the Christian camp. It brings with it many
of its own innovations, to be sure, but traceable ideolog-
ical influences have logically prepared the way for its
appearance. The xenophobia caused by its strange ideas
is, in many instances, unfounded.

Hence, though they are accused of being non-Christian, if not anti-Christian, the surprising fact is that the
young radical theologians are still strangely tied to
the Christian tradition. The umbilical cord is fearfully
stretched perhaps, but remains uncut. Their words may
be bold, shocking, and irreligious-sounding, but they all
reflect the Biblical heritage. This fact becomes more and
more obvious as one understands what they are saying
and grasps the overall implications of their thought. They
may speak, for example, as old-line atheists, but they
make it clear that it is a completely different kind of
atheism—a "Christian atheism," and those who find this
contradictory, if not ludicrous, are asked to enter the
new dialogue daringly as concerned *Christians* in order
to remain sensitive to new and vital *religious* ideas spun

off by the radical reorientation. Many outside the Christian religion would welcome them with open arms, yet the radical theologians adamantly insist that they are still Christians firmly grounded in the "essentials" of the Biblical tradition. Thus they confound both those within the church and those outside it. We do not believe that this declaration of theirs is taken seriously enough. We all can find reasons why; still the "death of God" theology will continue to be misunderstood, and perhaps unappreciated by many, until this point is made clear.

So, despite the discarding of a great deal of what they consider excess theological baggage from the musty cloakrooms of Christianity (thought of as the essentials by many), their new mufti is still hung on Christian pegs.

Van Buren, for instance, poses as a strict empiricist and has no patience with things supernatural, divine, otherworldly, or metaphysical, yet he still proclaims as central to his "gospel" the semimystical "contagion" of the spirit of Jesus, the catching of which frees all men from their intellectual, psychical, and social chains.

For Vahanian, the transcendent, living Spirit of the Biblical God, revealed fully by Jesus as the Christ, is still operative as a divine possibility within the arena of human history and the physical world, despite the dead God which contemporary Christianity idolatrously parades.

Altizer, seemingly the most radical of them all, mysticalizes Jesus and views his coming and death as a necessary dialectic stage of the Incarnate Word becoming immanent within the world as part of a cosmic process of constant creative renewal. He has even been accused of being a "literalist," for he strictly adheres to the Christian dogma "God was in Christ." He holds firmly to the idea that Christ died, and hence, through and in him, God died. God so loved the world that he gave himself to the world and died so that the world might have life. The resurrection is where Christianity went wrong, according to Altizer. It is a later Greek distortion, devoid of any historical evidence, which metaphysicalized the sacred back out of the world into which it had finally come once and for all through the incarnation. The eschatological movement of the Kingdom of God, or, as he calls it, the Dialectic of the Sacred, in which Christ plays the major role, is a concept which he finds more primordial and basic than the God concept.

Hamilton still clings to Jesus as Lord—the "man beside others"—and looks to him for inspiration and ethical guidance. One of the aims of radical theology, according to Hamilton, is to try to understand fully "that Jesus who appears in conjunction with the death of God."[11] The radical theologian has a "strange but compelling interest in the figure of Jesus."[12] Why he chooses this historical figure over other charismatic personalities as the paradigm of the religious (or secular) life is not easy at times even for Hamilton to say. But Jesus does remain the magnetic hub in his round of new theological adventures and allegiances.

Besides their programs for the "saving" of man according to definite suggested steps of thought and action, their secular variations of the eschatological views of history, and their acceptance of Jesus as Lord in some form or other, one can also detect in their writings a prophetic style and evangelistic zeal which is familiarly Christian. They all bring the "good news," the Word, which shall free us from past mythological "bliks," save us from deadly religiosity, make us more mature men fit for a "world come of age," and unite us with the full creative powers and new epiphanies of human existence. The old must be done away with, for now the new revelation has appeared: sacred profanities, secular optimism, technical efficiency, linguistic analysis, and *coincidentia opposi-*

torum! Here are the keys that unlock the "real" essence of "true" Christianity for an age, vouchsafed to them by the prophets Camus and Bonhoeffer, Blake and Hegel, Ayer and Hare.

The radical theologians may not be as arrogant in their claims as this analysis tends to make them; nor is it intended as a wry and premature value judgment (they may very well be correct). We are only attempting to show, however, what they themselves would freely admit: viz., that they regard themselves as legitimate Christian theologians working as best they know how within the framework of their religion, accepting the difficult but necessary task of reformulating what they regard as its vital truths for modern man.

On second look, the interested outsider's enthusiasm may well be premature; in many ways this may still be a family affair. Whether the dialogue with the secular elite continues in any kind of depth will depend entirely upon the future intents and efforts of these men.

II

That the "death of God" controversy is an unusual phenomenon in many ways seems obvious. However, we may ask ourselves whether this is reason enough to regard it as a theological event worth investigating. What are the reasons why we should seriously bother with it?

Professor Langdon Gilkey of the University of Chicago Divinity School — a renowned critic and interpreter of the "death of God" group—has cited five reasons why he believes "this new wind in theology" is important.

(1) It represents a definite new movement of theological thought, a new self-consciousness, with a

new starting point and something quite new to say.
. . . This vigor, originality and creativity is itself
worth our interest. (2) It represents an explicit
and potent rejection of the dominant neo-orthodox
"establishment" in theology that preceded it. Thus
its appearance and influence signalize the demise of
neo-orthodoxy as the ruling mode of theological
discourse, a not inconsiderable feat. (3) It represents within the circle of Christian theology the
mood and viewpoint of our present strongly "secular" age, an age that is metaphysically despairing
although it remains provisionally confident. Thus
while to me it does not express faithfully the Christian message, nevertheless it does present to us in
theological language and symbols the mind of
modern urban man — and this makes its serious
study a supremely significant task. (4) By representing this particular mood in modern life, a mood
despairing alike of coherence and meaning and of
the reality of religious faith, it creates an entirely
new situation for theological method, making provisionally irrelevant the starting points both of
liberal philosophy of religion and of revelationist
theology. (5) Finally, by asserting the death of God
and the need to construct a theology without Him,
it issues a fundamental challenge to the essential
structure of Biblical and Christian thought not only,
of course, about God, but also about Jesus, nature,
history and mankind—and for this reason, if for no
other, it must be comprehended and answered.[13]

Most of the members of Christendom welcomed the
news of the death of God as jubilantly as a hypochon-
driac on receiving a "get well soon" card, but the reasons
listed by Professor Gilkey and others for the importance
of this new theology only help to underline the significance of a serious study of it, not only by clergymen and

theologians but by laymen as well. Our agreement has
led to the editing of such a book as this.

III

Though the "death of God" theology swings mainly
about the two lodestars, Hamilton and Altizer, we have
included van Buren and Vahanian in this debate. This
has been done not only because they were orbiting in
the vicinity when the new star group was first sighted
in the radical constellation but because we discovered
that in seeking their own conceptual configurations, they
were repulsed and attracted by many of the same contemporary field forces. Their paths often intersect, even
though at other times they may move to polar opposites
of each other. Of the many representatives who consider
themselves attracted to, sympathetic with, or truly part
of this phase of radical theology, these four, we believe,
more legitimately represent the so-called "death of God"
controversy than others we have found. Also, van Buren
and Vahanian are included because in stating their own
involvement in the "new" theology and in distinguishing
their own meaning, or lack of meaning, of the phrase
"death of God," they clarify many of the key issues and
help the reader become cognizant of important variations
of theological thought currently at work.

This decision may seem a bit obstinate, however, in
the light of the fact that both van Buren and Vahanian
emphatically deny that they are "death of God" theologians. Van Buren, for instance, finds the whole thing quite
puzzling and has observed: "My identification with this
movement seems to me largely the work of journalists,
with at least an assist from a few others who ought to
know better. The implication of the way it has been
reported in the papers is that there is some tightly-knit,
integrated movement; this is simply not the case. My

name has been used in connection with several others, particularly Hamilton and Altizer. I can't find a great deal in common between us. . . . There are a number of theologians today who are working in ways which, to a certain sort of orthodoxy, would appear to be radical, but it would be a far larger number than just three or four mentioned in this connection." As to the "sad slogan 'God is dead,' " it is "logically absurd."[14]

Vahanian also repudiates the label. When asked if he was a "God is dead" theologian, he said: "Hell, no! It's hard enough to be simply a theologian. When anyone styles himself this or that theologian, I begin to worry. Labels can only serve to conceal the poverty of theology."[15]

Yet despite these specific denials, many have spied out authentic similarities which make their inclusion in the movement something more than a journalistic tour de force. For example, all four of these young theologians have written books and articles within the past four years that are vigorously iconoclastic, that reflect the open, tough-mindedness of our present secular age, that represent a repudiation of established orthodoxies, that take seriously some meaning of the phrase "death of God," or, as in the case of van Buren, the "death of God language." The work of all these men illustrates a courageous effort to discover new images of Christ and Christianity in the contemporary idiom, and seeks to create a new awareness within the church which demands a different beginning point for theology and a radically revised role of religion in life. Certainly these likenesses cannot be lightly dismissed as superficial.

Also, it is interesting to note that it was Vahanian who first used the phrase "death of God" again seriously as a theologian, reopening its use and giving it a new significance for our time. In his book *The Death of God*—published in 1961, two years before van Buren's *The Secular Meaning of the Gospel* and Altizer's *Mircea Eliade and the Dialectic of the Sacred*—he wrote:

Our culture is no longer transcendentalist but immanentist; no longer sacred or sacramental, but
secularistic or profane. This transition is explained
by the fact that the essentially mythological world
view of Christianity has been succeeded by a thoroughgoing scientific view of reality, in terms of
which either God is no longer necessary, or he is
neither necessary nor unnecessary: he is irrelevant
—he is dead.[16]

According to Vahanian, organized Christianity has mum-
mified its idea of God, fashioning him into an ethnic idol
which speaks a dead language and is totally irrelevant to
our culture. God is an "obstacle" today, rising between
man and the divine possibility; hence, he must be destroyed. If religion is to regain its former spiritual authenticity, it must rise from the ashes of the God of our post-
Christian era. It is true, in the last analysis, that "God
is *man's* failure" and that the "death of God" for Vahanian means "the death of those pagan deities that had
somehow survived in the Christian cultural conception of
God,"[17] but his ideas have that radical ring about them
which makes them vibrate with those of Hamilton and
Altizer. And in a real way, like them, he celebrates the
welcomed and necessary demise of the contemporary
Christian's God. (Vahanian's position vis-à-vis Hamilton
and Altizer is indicated in his article "Swallowed Up by
Godlessness" in this volume.)

As for van Buren, the similarities are more readily
recognizable, since he stands closer to Hamilton and
Altizer on the theological spectrum. This is evidenced in
the study made of the "God is dead" theology by Professor Gilkey. In his shrewd analysis of the writings of
Hamilton, Altizer, and van Buren, he discovers that there
are "five guiding theological principles" which "characterize the new theology in most of its present forms."

They are:

1. The unreality of God for our age; his absence from our current experience; the irrelevance and meaninglessness of all talk about him; the emptiness and actual harmfulness of any so-called relation to him; the impossibility of understanding our experience of evil if we try to believe in him—all of these leading to the one central assertion: God is dead.

2. The acceptance of the "world" and so of secular culture as providing the sole relevant environment, spiritual as well as physical, in which modern man can live. Thus the standards that that world recognizes as normative for inquiry are accepted as valid in theology, and, presumably, the goals of the world's life are regarded as normative ethically—though there appears to be some ambiguity in this latter regard.

3. The restriction of theological statements to what I can actually believe and accept myself, i.e., the principle of radical intellectual honesty, as opposed to accepting any statement as true on an authoritative or traditional ground (e.g. because it is "the Biblical view" or because "the Church has always maintained that . . .").

4. The centrality of the historical Jesus as he who ethically claims and guides us into the new worldly life.

5. The tendency to dispense with all mythological, suprahistorical, divine, eschatological or otherwise nonvisible and merely theological entities or categories, and the consequent confining of attention to this world and to what is directly visible, experienceable and verifiable within it.[18]

These tenets, which apply equally as well to van Buren's thought as to that of Hamilton and Altizer, legitimize, Professor Gilkey believes, his contention that they form the nucleus of a new theological movement—one that he feels, as we have seen, has begun an entirely new trend in doing theology. If he is correct, they also justify our inclusion of van Buren as part of the controversy.

It should be underscored again, however, that although the four representatives of the "death of God" theology included in this book are sometimes lumped together and referred to, for the sake of convenience, as the "radical" or "new" or "death of God" theologians, they all differ from one another, have their own styles, interests, and ideas, and that to read one is not to understand the thought of any of the others. Each must be evaluated in his own right. We are taking some liberties in referring to van Buren and Vahanian as "death of God" theologians, even though we feel that their inclusion is justified in a volume such as this.

IV

The basic features listed above by Professor Gilkey, plus the statements on the radical theology in the following selections, will help the reader locate these men on the theological map, so to speak. From the very beginning, there has been a felt need for a more responsible discussion of the issues involved and an answering of the many bothersome questions that have plagued people. This book attempts to do this. It attempts to inform the general public, too long nurtured on journalistic fare, what this new theological ferment is all about. It does so by placing in the readers' hands a group of articles, reviews, and letters that reflect not only the grass-roots reactions to the event but also the more thought-out, criti-

cal responses of the scholar. It particularly tries to avoid fanning any cultic flames or resorting to the clay-pigeon ruse of tossing a few of their more questionable ideas into the air for theological buffs to take potshots at. Even though the articles reflect a wide range of opinion, we believe they are responsible and serious statements.

We have not duplicated any source materials, even though we realize how advantageous and important this would be. There is no substitute for reading what the men themselves have written. But the primary documents are now readily available to the public.[19] Our main frustration was deciding which articles to include, since there are so many excellent ones—and more appearing every day. But space limitations prevented us from using all the material we would like to have included. There was a great deal of popular magazine and newspaper coverage which we surveyed, but we felt that this did not add to the depth of the discussion. We are aware, of course, that much theological writing at present is relevant to this expanding controversy (cf. Professor Trotter's article), but we have chosen to focus our attention on the intriguing stir of ideas elicited by the work of Altizer and Hamilton, and to a lesser extent of van Buren and Vahanian. This, after all, is what sparked the debate.

The format of the book represents our attempt to show different facets of the debate. Part I suggests some of the difficulties involved in understanding the meaning of the catchphrase "death of God." Part II includes the responses of various theologians to the work of four spokesmen most commonly identified with the debate, as well as what we hope to be a representative sampling of reactions to the "movement." Part III shifts the focus to the response of the public at large, as this is mirrored through the correspondence received by Professors Hamilton and Altizer. Part IV shows how three of the catalysts interpret the debate and how they project its ongoing significance for contemporary theology.

And now—the prolegomena ended—let the din of voices be heard!

NOTES

1. Thomas J. J. Altizer and William Hamilton, *Radical Theology and the Death of God* (The Bobbs-Merrill Company, Inc., 1966), p. ix.

2. Thomas J. J. Altizer, *The Gospel of Christian Atheism* (The Westminster Press, 1966), p. 9.

3. William Hamilton, "The Death of God," *Playboy*, August, 1966, p. 84.

4. Altizer and Hamilton, *Radical Theology*, p. 13.

5. *Ibid.*, p. 15.

6. *Ibid.*, p. 37.

7. *Ibid.*, p. 7.

8. William Hamilton, "The Death of God Theologies Today," *The Christian Scholar*, Vol. XLVIII (1965), p. 40.

9. Paul van Buren, *The Secular Meaning of the Gospel* (The Macmillan Company, 1963), p. 100.

10. Gabriel Vahanian, "Christianity's Lost Iconoclasm," *The Nation*, April 22, 1961, p. 354.

11. Altizer and Hamilton, *Radical Theology*, p. xii.

12. *Ibid.*

13. Langdon Gilkey, "The God Is Dead Theology and the Possibility of God Language." Mimeographed lectures given at The University of Chicago Divinity School, September, 1964, pp. 1–2.

14. From an interview reported in the Garrett Theological Seminary, *Forum*, No. 1 (1965–1966).

15. *Ibid.*

16. Gabriel Vahanian, *The Death of God* (George Braziller, 1961), p. xxxii.

17. Gabriel Vahanian, *Wait Without Idols* (George Braziller, 1964), p. 246 (italics added).

18. Gilkey, *op. cit.*, p. 14.

19. See also Altizer and Hamilton, *Radical Theology and the Death of God;* Altizer, *The Gospel of Christian Atheism;* van Buren, *The Secular Meaning of the Gospel;* and Vahanian, *The Death of God* and *Wait Without Idols.* All these works are available in paperback.

PART I

Some Questions
About
the "Death of God" Movement

Questions About the Death of Ace Davenport

Paul H. Wright

REFLECTIONS
ON THE GOD-KILLERS

THE VIEWPOINT of the "death of God" movement is hard to identify precisely, but it seems to boil down to one or a combination of the following propositions:

1. It is no longer *meaningful* to believe in the existence of God. This proposition cuts across several areas of our experience. (*a*) It is not meaningful to believe in God because such a belief is irrelevant to the problems of today's world. (*b*) It is not meaningful to believe in God because we do not have the language or symbolic categories to discuss him precisely or with genuinely communicable understanding. (*c*) It is not meaningful to believe in God because propositions about such a being are not subject to empirical verification by any form of controlled observation, and assertions that cannot be verified empirically are meaningless.

2. It is no longer *possible* to believe in the existence of God. Modern science has brought supernaturalism of any sort into disrepute. Things that are outside the scope of the "natural" and that are not, at least ideally, comprehensible by the methods of science simply do not happen.

3. It is no longer *necessary* to believe in the existence

of God. The "mysteries" of the universe have been or are being explained by scientific concepts and methods, so it is no longer necessary to postulate a God. And our ethical and moral structure finds a sufficient foundation and exemplar in Christ and the attitude of love and service he provided during his ministry; it adds nothing to assume that a transcendent God exists above and beyond that attitude.

These propositions, it is believed, point to the conclusion that God has died. But are the propositions intrinsically and inevitably sound, or do they rest upon some prior assumptions—a particular intellectual point of view —that might be called into question?

Time quotes Professor Altizer as follows: "We must recognize that the death of God is a historical event: God has died in our time, in our history, in our existence.". . . There are several possible interpretations of this quotation:

1. It could mean that people no longer take their belief in God seriously and no longer follow what they believe to be his will in their day-to-day conduct. Certainly there are vast numbers of people for whom God has ceased to exist. There are also vast numbers for whom he has never existed. On the other hand, there are vast numbers of people for whom he has not died, because they have believed and still believe in him and conscientiously seek and follow his will as they understand it. Thus, God has not died in any definitive sense.

2. The statement could mean that the systematic, empirically verified explanations of modern science have replaced God as an effective force in the universe. Here again, the power of the statement is weakened because of the many people for whom the achievements of science have not replaced God. Furthermore, this interpretation assumes that there is no God other than that which man himself "created" as a comfortable, catchall explana-

tion for phenomena that he does not understand. Further, this interpretation places far too much faith in the ability of science to provide "ultimate" answers; the inevitably partial and limited character of scientific explanation is overlooked. Here we might note the "humble" outlook of such scientific greats as Heisenberg and Einstein in forming our expectations about the kinds of answers science can provide.

3. The statement could mean that God and related Biblical concepts have outlived their relevance in that they do not offer any solutions to the widespread personal, social, economic, and political problems that beset today's world. In a sense, this interpretation combines the assumptions underlying the first two. (*a*) Since people no longer see or search for any relevance of Biblical concepts in the "real" world, God has lost his meaning, i.e., has died. (*b*) Since people now place more confidence in the effectiveness of so-called rational, nontheistic approaches to their problems, the God that they created to help solve those problems is no longer necessary or useful. Once more, there are many people who see a vital relevance of Biblical concepts for today's world and bend every effort to apply them. For many of these individuals, the systematic and empirically supported advances of the natural and behavioral sciences are considered to augment rather than to replace a God-centered orientation to the world and its problems. A conscientious Christian might well consider it not merely his prerogative but his *duty* to bring all his resources to bear upon the problems he faces. These resources certainly include his ability to understand and apply the contributions of science.

Can it be that the "death of God" writers have fallen into the trap (so common to purveyors of intellectual abstractions) of assuming that most people see the same and the only reality that they themselves see?

If the "death of God" position is, as seems most plausible, that God has died because men no longer find him believable or useful, then it must follow that God never really lived except in the imaginations of men. Apparently these men are saying, not that God has died, but that he never really had an independent existence. These theologians never say outright that there is no transcendent, independently existing God. Rather, the essence of their argument seems to be that we cannot know or comprehend God because of our limited perceptual, cognitive, and intellectual abilities. Moreover, such capabilities as we do have are inevitably confounded and trammeled by cultural forms and predefinitions. Here, the question seems not to be one of the nature of God but one of the nature of man as a knowing being. . . .

The "death of God" theologians seem to hail their admission of his demise as a breath of fresh air. Now that the theological air has cleared and Christianity has become thoroughly secularized, Christians can abandon doctrinal nonsense and express their Christianity in deep, heartfelt concern. The churchman will now be more free to demonstrate his Christian love by actually doing things for the economically deprived, for the undernourished millions, and for the ethnic and racial minorities in their struggle for equality. In other words, the Christian's concern will shift from an "otherworldly" focus to a "this-worldly" focus.

But is this a safe assumption? Will booting God out of our churches by trying to bury him necessarily mean that church people will show an increased concern for persons and social problems?

Are the "death of God" theologians really in a position to say that God has died? Or must they limit themselves to saying that within their own particular conceptual frameworks they have not been able to find him? What if they had made different assumptions or accepted the validity of different kinds of data or asked different questions? Would they still, of necessity, not be able to find God? Or does the question of whether God does or ever did exist still boil down to the age-old question, "To believe or not to believe"?

Persons of the more traditional, evangelical persuasion, using different assumptions, accepting different kinds of data, and holding to the validity of faith as a category of belief and experience, say that God does exist. We assume that God could and does reveal himself in various ways, including the written word as found in the Bible. We accept the life and works of Christ as, above all, the material expression of God's love and grace. To support our sometimes intangible-looking faith, we fall back upon the evidence of history. For example, something happened shortly after the crucifixion of Christ to bring about a miraculous revitalization of his depressed, dejected, and utterly defeated disciples. Something happened that we remember as the "Day of Pentecost" that stimulated a social, ethical, and religious movement that has had a tremendous impact upon the world. Is this sort of evidence sufficient reason for believing in God and in Christ as the Son of God? We naïve Christians think so, and we believe.

Fred M. Hudson

FOUR MEANINGS
OF "THE DEATH OF GOD"

A NEW SCHOOL OF THEOLOGY has emerged in the past year, often called—largely at the insistence of its critics—"The Death of God Theology." It is a small movement of young theologians who have independently been appealing to Christians to make theological sense out of what our culture as a whole decided (functionally if not cognitively) sometime ago, namely, that the Judeo-Christian God, who used to be confessed as the Alpha and Omega of all history, is experienced today as a nonentity; a powerless, fading memory; a blank, gone reality; a meaningless term.

Yet these young radicals had barely hinted at some of the themes which might constitute a theology without God before both the religious establishment and the man on the street issued amazingly premature protests, shrugging it off as a form of irresponsible extremism.

The main tenor of the protests from the professional theologians is that the new theology is "arrogant," i.e., claiming what cannot be claimed by man, that *God* is

Reprinted by permission from *motive*, April, 1966. Copyright ©
1966 by the Division of Higher Education of The Methodist
Church.

THE "DEATH OF GOD" MOVEMENT

dead. The new theology is brushed aside as little more than an adolescent publicity stunt of a few bored theologians. At most it is seen as a new form of "idolatry" which sets man up as a golden calf. But is it any less arrogant or idolatrous to say that God is alive? Perhaps only agnostics can be humble men of faith. Surely there are better lines of criticism!

The main tenor of the protests from the man in the street is that the new theology is "atheistic," an un-American flurry of a few extremists. Anyone familiar with the sociology of religion in America knows that most Americans say they believe in God even if they are not practicing or knowledgeable adherents to any religious tradition. Belief in God is still a part of being American; thus the so-called "atheism" of the new theologians is associated with foreign (alas! even Communist) influences. Even a culture which operates cognitively without reference to God does not want theologians to say God is not available, even to the religions that are not practiced! Is it too much to ask for an understanding of the difference between a-theism (not-theism) and atheism (anti-theism)? The former is a confession of faith without God, a possible function of theology; the latter is an opposition to faith and God, a manifestation of some allegiance other than theology.

The "death of God" theology builds on the cultural criticism which theologians have utilized for the past forty years to attack the religious presuppositions of man and to illustrate the poverty of all attempts to prove the existence of God. Revealed theology, in particular, consistently has maintained a negative theme regarding man's various attempts at becoming godlike. The "death of God" theology moves from these negative criticisms of the knowledge of God in human experience to an analogous criticism of the belief in God through theological confessions. . . .

This radical reduction in the role of theology accounts for three meanings of the "death of God": psychological, sociological, and ontological.

The *psychological* meaning of the "death of God" is that man has lost his inner awareness of God. Human self-understanding now proceeds without a God hypothesis. There seems to be no part within us that needs God, draws us to him, or responds to him. In this sense, to say "God is dead" is to say that religious experience is dead. The psychological meaning of the "death of God" is that many men have lost the capacity to know "God" through human experience. In other words, the first meaning of the "death of God" is the death of an awareness within our finitude of anything beyond finitude. It is a psychological or existential comment upon us, not a description of the nonexistence of God.

The *sociological* meaning of the "death of God" is that the central consciousness-shaping institutions of our society no longer utilize or foster a God consciousness. The political, economic, and educational institutions which used to convey and confirm the presence of God no longer do so. In other words, to say "God is dead" sociologically is to say that Christendom is dead. The Christian West is no more, for the institutions that shape men's mentality no longer rest upon theological premises. We are living in a post-Christian era. The sociological meaning of "God is dead" is a comment on our social situation, not a comment on God as such. However, it should be increasingly clear that whatever God may be in himself, if man cannot know him psychologically or sociologically, God cannot *mean* very much. It is a short step to saying, with Sartre: whether God exists or not, he is of no use to us.

The *ontological* meaning of the "death of God" is that there are no symbols today which convey an ultimate meaning for our spatiotemporal existence. We do not know how to refer to or how to express a unifying reality or "Being" who "acts in history to judge and forgive." The former tools of philosophy of religion—that God is a predicate, or that God language is metaphorical or analogical—have been outmoded like spinning wheels and geocentric cosmologies, for they rest on some ontic base within our experience, inexpressible in our language. This ontic base is precisely that which we seem to have lost. To say that God is dead ontologically is to say that we have no words or symbols which *mean* God. This may only be a comment on our language and symbols rather than upon God. However, if we cannot speak of him, then even if we "believe" in him, he is consciously a problem to us, not a reality.

It is important to realize that this theological critique of the human situation is not new with the "death of God" theology. One glimpses similar formulations in the psalms, and in the writings of Pascal, Kant, Kierkegaard, and Dostoevsky, to mention but a few. Barth, Brunner, and Tillich all took this development very seriously, interpreting "God is dead" to mean "the idolatries of man are dead." The death of God as the death of idolatries, with its psychological, sociological, and ontological thrusts, has been a useful polemic for theologians in the past forty years, as a comment upon man and man's culture, but not as a theological comment upon the Christian faith itself.

The new twist in the "death of God" theology is that even theology must reformulate itself without a God premise. Neo-Reformation theologians have stopped short of this final step by employing a doctrine of revelation, a *sui generis* source of divine activity. God is made known by disclosing himself *in faith alone,* they have said, as the Wholly Other who reveals his humanity in Jesus Christ to those who have faith, or as the ground of being who is believed when man experiences the limits of his finitude. The church remains as that peculiar historical community with "eyes of faith" to see God active in secular history, even in secular man's unbelief. Man is not expected to know God as he knows other objects, but rather to respond to God as he is hidden in the secular. Neo-Reformation theology has viewed God as being incomprehensible to our objectifying consciousness, yet present in ordinary history: as he reveals himself (I am what I am) and as we "believe" through the frame of reference (theology) and the forms of liturgical-servant life (the church).

Furthermore, many theologians have continued, man's life apart from faith in God is filled with restless anxiety and despair. Even the "death of God" literature up until now has helped underscore this point. Nietzsche wrote a haunting story of a madman who ran into a village square shouting, "God is dead!" It took a madman to make such a claim! A character in Dostoevsky's *The Possessed* says, "If God is dead, then everything is permitted." Existential themes have reinforced this analysis, and such a portrayal of the condition of man without God has made a doctrine of revelation more plausible. A Camus character asks: "Can one become a saint without God?" And André Malraux wrote, "The nineteenth century faced the question, 'Is God dead?'; the twentieth century now faces the question, 'Is Man dead?'" The two questions seemed to go together, and the doctrine of revelation was an answer to such an analysis.

However, the new "death of God" theologians do not feel that man is forever restless and despairing apart from God, and they contend that a doctrine of revelation adds neither faith nor knowledge to our given, secular patterns of existence. There are Biblical tools which are useful, but not the doctrine of God. And when God's death is entertained seriously *in theology itself*, a radically historical concept of man and his salvation emerges.

Thus, the new theology is based on a *new doctrine of man* and on a *new doctrine of salvation*. Man is viewed with new optimism, as a good part of the profane order, with no need for the sacred in either faith or knowledge. Salvation is viewed as a style or pattern of historical activity: *in, by,* and *for* the secular.

Is not contemporary man finding a new kind of unity in life, not in the knowledge of God or in faith in God (a doctrine of revelation), but in the common secularity of life and thought as conveyed in the ordinary language and concerns of the newspapers, movies, TV, art, love, and politics of our time? Is it possible that making *any* appeals to God—through a doctrine of revelation as well as through psychological, sociological, and ontological claims to divine knowledge—in an age so completely secularized only divides our lives, our minds, and our world? Is it possible that trying only to fathom the meaning of the world as we experience it without any appeals to God—through knowledge or faith—more closely parallels what God in the Bible kept requiring of his people: to be responsible in and for the world? If, culturally speaking, we have edged God out of our understanding of the world, has not the emergence of a new basis for human wholeness in the secular process itself edged out the meaningfulness of our recourse to God through a doctrine of revelation? Is it possible for us to be faithful in our handling of the creative process before us without using God as a working hypothesis in either our knowledge or our faith?

The new proposal is close to Camus' statement:

> When the throne of God is overturned, the rebel realizes that it is now his responsibility to create the justice, order and unity that he sought in vain with his own condition, and in this way, to justify the fall of God. (*The Rebel,* p. 25.)

But whereas for Camus this meant abandoning Christianity for an agnostic humanism, some of the new theologians are suggesting that not only is it possible to make theological sense out of the world without referring to God: it is the new essence of Christianity, the message of the church for our time. These men do not believe theology should employ a doctrine of revelation in order "to keep alive the rumor of God."

They suggest that the "death of God" has a *fourth* meaning, a theological meaning. Who are these men? Certainly Bonhoeffer and Robinson hint at the new development. So does Harvey Cox in the last chapter of *The Secular City*. But the three most vocal members of this new, radical theology are Thomas J. J. Altizer of Emory, William Hamilton of Colgate Rochester Divinity School, and Paul van Buren of Temple University. While it must be said that there is no simple agreement among these men, three themes are at least persistent.

First, the death of God as a theological concern means that God is a problem for us, not a reality. Both our knowledge of God and our confession of him as Lord are problematical. For forty years now we have juggled God from self-revealed to transcendent to hidden to absent to eclipsed. It is a short step from these maneuvers which keep our cognition of God in abeyance to saying that even "in faith" God is gone from us. For these men, it is of no theological use to call upon God or to believe in him. Again this is a predication of our theological experience, not a statement about God as such; but there is a theological function in speaking this way. It shifts our attention from God to man, from revelation to world. It takes a metaphor as strong as the death image to convey a sense of finality, meaning that theology needs to begin with some premise other than a faith statement about God. These men contend that theology can only begin negatively about God, but that such a negation will prove to be creative in the fresh ways it allows us to interpret the world, as *Christians*. The psychological, sociological, and ontological experience of the death of God has led some Christians to experience the death of God theologically. This does not mean we should stop being Christians, or stop being concerned with the future possibility of God. It means we need to see if Christianity without a God confession has other positive meanings for our present lives.

Second, since the verdict about God is that he is not available, the theological burden must be borne by some other aspect of theology. For van Buren and Hamilton, the usual focal point is Jesus, the man for others. The Christian is one who learns from Jesus the identity and worth of his neighbors. If God is for us a central problem, Jesus is the central interpreter of the human situation. Jesus' way of responding to others around him provides us today with a perspective on how to respond in faithfulness to those around us. He is the model of what human life is to be. So, if one speaks of the death of God, he speaks of the life of Jesus. Altizer has a different focus, that of eschatological mysticism. By willing the death of God, not as a metaphor but as an event, Altizer believes we open ourselves to the deep mystery of profane history, which is moving toward the end of all polarities.

Third, the Christian faith for our time is fundamentally a form of humanism, not theism. That is, the focus of faith is not God but a faithful or responsible handling of human relationships. And the way in which the Christian understands his humanism is not by idealizing or idolizing man as in other forms of humanism, but by following the clues offered by Biblical man, by Jesus, and by the saints of the church.

Christianity is the discernment of an inner, humanizing dialectic or style in the historical process, the awakening of some men to the recovery of manhood available to all men. It is seeking deliverance from bondage as Moses sought it; seeking to forgive one's brothers as Joseph forgave his; seeking to be judged by others as Israel was judged time and time again; seeking to be humanized with Jesus in the feeding of the hungry. In short, it is learning from Biblical man's handling of history without resorting to his rationale. It is loving God's world without appealing to God as a special source of love. The claim is that Christianity today is one form of humanism, based upon a particular history with particular emphases, and valid as such.

Where does all this leave the church? It is too early to tell. Can we proclaim God's death, or only our death to God? Can we have Jesus apart from the Father on whom he said he depended? Can we be humanists apart from the trust in transcendent judgment and forgiveness? Is this a new form of apologetics or a reformulation of dogmatics? Or is it only the last gasp of theological disillusionment? It is too early to tell. Perhaps it will lead to a revival of an understanding of God in terms of natural rather than revealed theology. Perhaps it will foster a new form of Biblical criticism based on the resurrected tools of the history and phenomenology of religion.

There is a danger that too many Americans will equate the "death of God" theology (which might more properly be called "radical theology," since the death of God is only the beginning of its more positive claims) with simple atheism or with a new form of idolatry. Most of the initial criticism has been along these lines. What is being claimed is much more: *a reformulation of the essence of Christianity.*

Interpretive Articles:
The Response
of the Theological
Community

Warren L. Moulton

APOCALYPSE IN A CASKET?

T HE ICONOCLASTIC cracking and breaking among the young radical theologians is exciting, and we must admire this latest attempt among theologians to discover personal credibility for all of us. These davids have slain goliath, god of the pious philistines—but getting the neck cut and the head raised on a spear is tough, messy business. Some of the davids wield two-edged swords and no doubt wear plastic aprons. And they are all determined to get in there and chop, since at this point the squad is small. In William Hamilton's "The Shape of a Radical Theology" (*The Christian Century,* Oct. 6), I thought for a moment that we saw the gory head of God go up on the spear. But these are beginnings, and what we saw was only dry-run papier-mâché. There will be dissenters, but the author's attempt to "see if there is anybody out there" will at the same time bring recruits.

However, there was something about the very character of Hamilton's article that revealed how insubstantial the "death of God" thesis is at this point. There

From the November 17, 1965, issue of *The Christian Century.* Copyright 1965 Christian Century Foundation. Reprinted by permission.

seemed to be in the author a mood of cynical resignation, a the-whole-world-is-my-ashtray attitude. So that some of us who have lately listened to the pallbearers around God's box wondered again: How much do you really care about any of it?

The radical theologians have been making noises like heroes, and some of us have cheered. We have read their literature, gathered our students to hear them speak, discussed them over coffee with our colleagues. And we have agreed that these are exciting minds. They suggest a new freedom with dignity, and this sounds good after the rigidity of neo-orthodoxy in the face of revolutions. We stand like beggars waiting further revelations. Then we receive another release, and its picture of the "shape of a radical theology" leaves us feeling like urbanites trying to read bird tracks. We are confused, and we have questions.

Those who tell us that God is dead must realize that for the most part theology is thus also extinguished. They have dissolved the center of reality. Since God is dead, what can we make of the rest of it? We cannot merely enjoy in Jesus only what is historically there (after editing, etc.): one great man with some good ideas and a lot of courage, like a few other people we know.

Furthermore, must we not concern ourselves about a new ethic? We have a good residue, and men are intelligent; there is very little to stop us from creating a modern, fast, urban great society. Besides, God has long since ceased to touch most people vitally. He has not even affected personal habits as he might have a few short puritan years ago: people quit smoking because of government reports, and no foul-minded little cleric is going to reduce religion to not smoking because of something about the body being the temple of God. Isaiah tells us that the Temple was filled with smoke and the Lord appeared. Well, he waited too long. So we quit the tobacco *and* the Lord.

I

If it is true that what the radical theologian is saying is the direction of things in our time, that this is truly all there is left, perhaps we who are interested in their words might make a few suggestions.

First, we would ask of these men humility rather than resignation, compassion rather than indulgence. Is the proud talk of cult and journal put together in the name of the new radical theologians necessary for dialogue at this time, or might it wait? When some of us hear these "death of God" voices we have a feeling that we are dealing with successful, highly polished young brains with a good grain, seated in a cosmic bridge game with a young, cynical audience looking on. They play with a grin, with perfect finesse. They may even put us off with talk of being embarrassed because their shadow was showing on a TV god-game quiz, and of how this has given them a psychic zipper snag. We hear these cool, sophisticated, prophetic voices, and perhaps we long for a touch of the spirit of priest and pastor.

Second, it would appear that without our faith in the reality of God we can know little or nothing about the love which we call *agapē*. Jesus demonstrated love in a most definitive fashion in his own life and death and in his commission of his disciples—and the quality and nature of his love rested on his faith in a living God. The Fourth Gospel suggests that love is what the notion of God is all about. Paul said that love is all that finally matters in man's communication with the realm of his reality. Does not *agapē* as discovered in Christ demand a living God?

One may frequently be in dialogue *about* this *agapē*-God. That is a fascinating theological game. But unless one believes that God is alive in the world which we address and hear, unless one believes that other men are talking with and about this same God, not only is reality shattered but God is removed from our remembering, our imagining, and our telling, and is put beyond all our seeking. Is not *agapē*-love as discovered in Christ fraudulent if we do not also believe in Christ's God?

This love is love that does not stop; this is the love we use to describe God. And this is the most significant thing we can say about the love learned from Jesus: We have received through him a commandment from God not to quit loving, in order that our brother may escape the sickness that comes when one absolutely quits loving or concludes when and where his love stops. For a man to believe in a love that stretches forward without end to every brother in all conditions, he must trace it to its source in the infinity of man's reality which is God. Beyond any notion of the end of love is God. If God is not there, my love becomes selective, tentative, budgeted, changes character to fit my mood. For most of us the word to love without ceasing must come from God, else our humanity rejects the word.

The work of living now can be attempted only if man believes that there is a love at the heart of reality, and that despite the threat or fact of death the transcendent nature of things is love, that man as creature searching for the Creator of this love will survive. Are creature and Creator laughably one?

Evidence that God lives is there in the search for this never-ending love which we preach. I am alive only in my searching; when I quit, then I begin to die. If God is dead, will not man quit searching and loving? Perhaps instead of announcing the death of God, I should simply register the death of myself and my brother. For if God is dead, the search for *agapē* stops, and man dies. Is Beckett right when he says, in *Waiting for Godot*: "God died in the 19th century and man disappeared in the 20th"?

II

Third, since Hamilton calls for optimism, he obviously does not think that man is dead. The "radical theology" does not have a central doctrine of sin; it sees a spirit of optimism as one of its important motifs. It may be only semantics, but optimism seems just a comic version of what has been called Christian joy. For the joy that was set before him Christ endured the cross. With the arrival of optimism and the departure of this particular joy, a central nerve is frayed. More than pure knowledge, dogma, or mystical faith, the joy of which Paul wrote expresses the character of the Christian faith. We associate such joy with our Lord's overcoming the world (perhaps a coming over to the world in a new and profound way?). It was his peace in Gethsemane. It was his poise before Pilate. It was the spirit of the early church. And it comes with a man's sense of the presence of God. Can it *be,* unless God *is?* Where God truly *is, there* is joy. Was God in Christ, reconciling the world joyously, even through the agony of incarnate dying?

Admittedly, there is little left on the human scene to make the human spirit sing. History is open-ended, and every suggested finale is grim. We are hysterical at the thought of too many people and not enough food. The human kaleidoscope is changing; white is only a color for mixing. In every philosopher's nicely wrapped package we find the bomb. Our music is a dirge. Art depicts our pathos. A crucified Lord rots in the tomb, while the pep-rally revivals continue to call for the blood-bucket brigade. Our priests are content to throw dirt upon the dead.

What shall we say? It appears to be either the circus or prayers, hysterics or meditation, ravage or the cloister. But optimism sounds frivolous; joy sticks. Optimism appears to forget the news; joy will embrace the leper. Only this kind of joy can make it now. Without joy we are the candlesnuffers and the lamp breakers of the world. Our "Hallelujah Chorus" is an organ grinder's tune unless we too can really come over to the world, expecting gritty pain, man's flight from God and his warm pool of pity— and come over in joy. Optimism begs; joy thrives in barrenness. Can we find this joy in the freedom of the determined barrenness of God's death?

III

Finally, with the demise of theology, our Christology seems to deflate, to leave us with a depressingly sick Christ. If Christ presumed God, his motivation is now totally suspect, his words brittle as glass; and his crucifixion looks increasingly like something he really deserved. Is this where we must go?

Says Hamilton: "I am drawn, and I have given my allegiance. There may be powerful teachings elsewhere, more impressive and moving deaths. Yet I have chosen him and my choice is not arbitrary nor is it anxiously made to avert the atheist label. It is a free choice, freely made." This is good, but it seems to play to an ignoble dwarf in us that says, "I know it is silly, but this is the way I feel." Such an attitude can be as emotionally dependent as a billygraham convert, as irrational as a snake handler; it makes the existential leap little more than Elizabeth crossing the muddy street on Raleigh's coat.

Can we stick by Jesus just because we like the toys in his sandbox? Jesus is still the nicest guy we know, and we will not run away—but is this enough for a viable Christology? Obviously not. It has the ring of a final honesty, but it is more a jesus-jingle than a confession of discipleship. Yet we ask if any of us really offers any more of himself.

Is the good, solid humanism which Hamilton suggested not better, a more honorable discharge from the faith? If one is going, why not walk right past the bier and say: "It was great, Man, but that wavelength is full of static. See you around the god-quad, of course." In Hamilton's confession we are left with the feeling that the Jesus myth is poetically, mythically useful for a man finding his perspective—but let's sleep in on Sunday.

However, because of the element of truth I hear in Hamilton and others like him, I would suggest this: Jesus was proclaimed as the fulfillment of prophecy; the long-imagined Messiah had come. The contemporary Christ is somehow the fulfillment of each theological man's prophecy regarding his savior. The prophetic in each man is his cry of humanity. Gathering bits and pieces from his reality, the image of a savior forms in his soul. The image of the Savior Christ transcends the bread, wine, and nails of his flesh, and the whole myth of man healed and God healing in Jesus remains as the Word of salvation to many and the promise to all. But the image of the Savior Christ must also transcend each man's own trapped condition. Although he comes to me, I cannot limit him to my condition. He identifies with me and moves on to another who has also prophesied his coming. God in Christ invades humanity and each man; but he must be permitted to escape humanity and each man if he is to be alive and contemporary for every age. Jesus may be back there with the Caesars unless a new Christology fashions him in the prophetic vision of this day, unless he comes over to *this* world and saves us. And if men will not permit this of today's theologians, the churchman will continue to speak and not care, to hear and not believe.

Theodore Runyon, Jr.

THOMAS ALTIZER
AND THE FUTURE OF THEOLOGY

N ATTEMPTING TO CLARIFY and assess critically the contribution of Thomas J. J. Altizer to theological discussion in our time, I shall employ a rather broad descriptive typology. Like all typologies, it will not do justice to all the factors, but its use will be defensible, I trust, if it makes a few of the main issues more clear.

Generally speaking, man has expressed his consciousness of divine reality in two basic ways. One of these we shall call "the way of *identity*," the other, "the way of *distinction*." According to the way of identity, man intuits himself and the divine as one, at least on the ultimate level; the way of distinction insists on distinguishing the reality of God from that of man at every level.

The "way of identity" is by far the more venerable and the more universal. It can be observed as operative in some of religion's most subtle and highly developed forms as well as in its most primitive manifestations. Whether primitive or sophisticated, however, the way of identity views reality as monolithic. The gods do not have their reality independently from the world but rather are the personification of world forces. Man himself, at least in the primitive forms of this approach, does

Previously unpublished.

not differentiate himself from the cosmos of which he is a part. He understands himself, his society, and his daily life as an integral part of a world which is in its totality *sacred*. Though there may be areas of his life or his world which take on special sanctity for cultic purposes, these sacred acts and places only represent the whole of life, the whole of his world. The divine is intuited fundamentally; therefore, not as a separate object (even though the worshiper may be surrounded by idols) but as that which permeates his whole existence. Because the divine is continuous with the world, access to the divine requires no mediation. Insofar as he is able to penetrate through the superficial and actually illusory levels of his existence, man finds himself to be in immediate touch with the holy. He participates ecstatically in the ultimate principle of the universe.

Moreover, man intuits this ultimate principle to be unmoved and unmoving. This is why he joyfully embraces it as the answer to the problem of his own existence, plagued as he is by insecurity, instability, and change. By means of his participation in the ultimate unmoving, unchanging reality, he is assured of that which is permanent in the midst of change. The enlightened man is thus able to recognize "change" as a deficient mode of being and finally illusory.

The way of identity, therefore, presents us with a monolithic approach to reality in which the gods, the world, and man all have an ultimate identity in the infinite, unchanging One which is All.

In contrast, the approach to the reality of the divine which I have termed "the way of *distinction*" draws a fundamental difference between God and the world, and exercises considerable effort to maintain this difference in the face of recurring tendencies to weaken or erase it. The typical way of asserting the distinction is by differentiating between Creator on the one hand and creature and creation on the other. "Creature" and "creation," even when raised to their highest powers, are still qualitatively distinct from Creator, according to this view. To quote Kierkegaard, there is an "infinite qualitative difference between man and God." The divine is not available to man as an immediate principle either within himself or his world. Rather, contact between the human and the divine is characteristically understood as being initiated from the side of the divine and involves an interaction between the divine and the human which is analogous to interpersonal relations. Indeed, the way of distinction would assert that, strictly speaking, "relations" can exist only where there is difference, and thus it would be improper to speak of "relation" within an identity context. For things which, at the point of their mutual interaction, are intuited as identical are not related, they are simply one.

Having noted the fundamental contrast between these approaches in their understanding of the nature of the divine-human link, we are not surprised to find that the way of distinction has a contrasting view of change. "Relation" is understood on the model of an event in time and space; that is, it has a reality which transcends man as well as involving him, and it occurs in the flux of history. Time-space existence, therefore, as the arena of man's contact with the divine, is not a deficient mode of being, it is not illusory. It is just as "real" as is God himself. It is where salvation takes place.

This means, however, that the God who is interacting with man in this time-space dimension is just as involved in history and change as is man. He is not above the historical flux but commits himself to it; and he is known in the midst of the flux not as the static, unmoving absolute but as the Faithful One of Israel.

The Kingdom of God which Jesus proclaimed, and which he may have sensed as dawning in his own ministry, was the Kingdom of this kind of God and was to be realized in a new history. His ministry may have had ecstatic overtones, but one thing is clear, he conceived of the Kingdom fundamentally as the reconstituting of all relationships: God with man, man with his fellowmen, man with the world.

The way of distinction, therefore, puts a positive valuation on the time-space continuum and, though it sees divine redemption as the *remaking* of history into something new, it cannot conceive of divine-human interaction in other than historical terms which preserve the qualitative difference between God and man.

Now let us attempt to locate Altizer's contribution to the future of theology in terms of this typology. He is seeking to do a very daring thing, one that has exciting and far-reaching implications.

I believe it is accurate to say that Altizer's roots are in the identity approach. That approach has, in the past, spoken most directly to his religious sensibilities. The immediate awareness of the Holy, the *mysterium tremendum*, ecstatic participation in the Sacred: this is language he can understand and with which he can identify, as is evidenced by his first book, *Oriental Mysticism and Biblical Eschatology*. More recently, however, Altizer has become at least partially dissatisfied with "the way of identity." Why? Because in its traditional forms it is unable to put a positive value on the historical process. As a result, it can neither take the problem of evil in history seriously nor affirm a redeemed future in time. Christianity, however, does both. In Christianity the problem of evil, for example, is not an illusion which is to be escaped but the occasion for responsibility in this world, for struggle and for ultimate victory. The present and future have significance according to Christian faith because they are the plane on which God is working out his will. God has a stake in history. He has a destiny.

Now we are in a position to see more clearly the uniqueness and daring of Altizer's theological venture. He stands in two theological worlds. He is unwilling to

give up either, because he has a vision of combining
both of them. This is not a matter of syncretism, he asserts, for the combination is demanded by the deepest
religious insight of both approaches. What I have presented as two contradictory approaches he feels to be
dialectically related. The way of identity, the way traditionally associated with oriental mysticism, must be
completed by a world-affirming involvement in history.
Its world denial, if understood dialectically in terms of
the "coincidence of opposites," is actually world-affirming,
he insists. And this potential for world affirmation ought
to be given theological expression, which the East has
not as yet done. Precisely here lies the Western contribution, for only in the West, and—in spite of the fact
that it was implicit in the Christian gospel—only in our
time, has "change" become something no longer to be
feared but rather to be welcomed as the bringer of hope
and the unfolding of the divine (Hegel). "Modern man
is the first to live so fundamentally out of the *future,*"
says Gerhard Kruger, "that for him the *new* as such has
a magical attraction."[1] If it can be demonstrated that
world affirmation is implicit within the way of identity,
the Eastern approach need no longer place a negative
value on change but can learn from the West that there
is no necessary conflict between change and the divine,
nor is there any need to view the dimension of the sacred
as antagonistic to the phenomenon of change.

Equally important, however, are the implications for
Christianity. The Christian proclamation will be
complete only as it recognizes that the way of distinction
was only a passing stage in the divine evolution. It was
a projection of the alienation and repression which man
experiences in his society. But now through the insight
of the true inheritors of the Christian gospel, seers as
Blake, Hegel, and Nietzsche, this projection can be recognized for what it is. It need no longer victimize and

repress, for it is in the process of dying away. History is moving toward the ultimate dissolution of the distinction between God and man and a merging of the two in the new godmanhood of the eschatological age.

This vision of a new way of identity Altizer sees as inherent in the true meaning of the incarnation. Theology in the past, he argues, has not taken with radical seriousness the claim, in Phil. 2:7, that Christ, in entering the world, "emptied" himself (Greek, *kenōsis*) of his divinity, pouring out his divinity into the world and assuming full and complete humanity. With this one act of self-giving, namely, the life and death of Jesus, God willed to join himself with the world, so that from henceforth he is no longer to be found in the heavens—the transcendent, domineering God is dead—but must be found where he wills to be found, that is, in his world.

It has taken Christianity nineteen hundred years to discover that the God who is distinct from man and the world no longer exists, says Altizer. The seers of the nineteenth century finally grasped the fact, and now it is breaking through to the masses. (It is in this dual sense that Altizer wants to insist that "God has died in our time, in our history, in our existence.") His point is that this death of God was implicit from the beginning in the Christian proclamation, for it was a death willed by God himself. Though we are only now beginning to realize it, as our awareness of this fact increases we move into new possibilities for becoming sensitized to the life of God in his incarnate form, that is, in the world Christologically viewed. Our eyes are opened to his epiphany, and we begin to see the dawning of that Kingdom which complete union with the divine in this world will bring, namely, the new humanity, the divine humanity, our being remade in the image of Christ, our identity with the truly Sacred.

Anyone who is serious about the task of theology in

our day cannot but appreciate the breadth of Altizer's vision and the ambitiousness of his undertaking. If he succeeds, he will have accomplished what no other theologian has satisfactorily done: he will have joined the characteristic religious ways of the East and the West together in one consistent approach, albeit on an Eastern base but with strong Western contributions. This accomplishment would have consequences of the utmost importance for missiology and ecumenism. Thus, regardless of one's attitude toward Altizer's thought, there is no denying its seminal significance.

Let me now indicate, however, what I consider to be the chief difficulties in his approach. I shall mention just two.

My first question has to do with Altizer's interpretations of Biblical passages and of traditional Christian doctrines. Is it legitimate, on Biblical and historical grounds, to make the kind of nondialectical use of traditional language which Altizer does? He employs (a) the *kenōsis* passage in Philippians, (b) the doctrine of the incarnation, and (c) the eschatological message of Jesus to justify dissolving the distinction between God and the world, bringing God into identity with the world in a way which, though initially dialectical, is ultimately thoroughly monistic.

Altizer's interpretation of the self-emptying (*kenōsis*) of Christ as the merging of God with the world may be defensible if one is reading Paul via Hegel and Blake. But if one is attempting instead to get at Paul's own orientation, then it would seem that for Paul the most basic sin of man is that he confuses God with the world, the Creator with the creation:

Claiming to be wise, they became fools, and exchanged the glory of the immortal God for images resembling mortal man or birds or animals or reptiles.... They exchanged the truth about God for a lie and worshiped and served the creature rather than the Creator. (Rom. 1:22-25.)

How can a reading which eliminates the distinction between Creator and creation claim to do justice to Paul's theological intention?

Nor did the historical doctrine of the incarnation intend to provide a basis for a dissolution of the difference between man and God. Even in Chalcedon's tortured attempts to bend rational language to serve the cause of paradox it is evident that in the description of the new humanity, Jesus Christ, the God-man, the distinction between the divine and the human is to be maintained:

We apprehend this one and only Christ... in two natures;... without confusing the two natures, without transmuting one nature into the other.... The distinctiveness of each nature is not nullified by the unity.[2]

Regardless of what one thinks about the adequacy of this formula, it is clear that the classic doctrine of the incarnation cannot be construed as supporting, even eschatologically, a dissolving of the distinction between God and man.

Finally, Jesus' own apocalyptic message can scarcely be credited with pointing toward the elimination of the Creator-creature distinction, for his was the proclamation of the inbreaking of the reign of the *Lord*. And "Lord" and "servant," even when transmuted by Jesus into "Father" and "son," remain distinct, noninterchangeable categories. In raising the term "son" to the highest power, we still have "son" and not "father." To be sure, the inbreaking of the Kingdom meant the transvaluing of all previous religious and cultural values; but this transvaluation was one of completely reconstituted relationships, not one of mystical identity. For Jesus, the eschaton means that God will be God, and man will be man and not attempt to be God anymore. True creaturehood will be restored, which is at the same time full humanity. And thus there will be peace, joy, life!

It would seem to me, therefore, that the use Altizer makes of Jesus' eschatological message, Paul's notion of the self-emptying of Christ, and the traditional doctrine of the incarnation, is suspect in the light of their historical contexts and original intentions.

My second question has to do with the nature and extent of secularization and the response appropriate to it.

Contrary to the impression some may have received, Altizer is not uncritical of the process of secularization. True, he warmly greets the process insofar as it is releasing persons in our time from their bondage to the transcendent God (who in his dead and negated form is better identified as "Satan"). Yet, unlike those who might uncritically embrace the "secular city," Altizer recognizes that secularization is a very mixed blessing. Why? Because it destroys not only false religion but any sensitivity to the Sacred as well. The technological world is no new savior. It is dull, flat, boring, and finally demonic, because it prevents the realization of that new humanity which is only possible where the Holy is present and participated in. Therefore, for Altizer, secularization is *good* insofar as it destroys that God who is different from man, but *bad* insofar as it also eliminates the religious instinct, the awareness of the Sacred, that divine dimension of experience which is intuited as identical with man's own ultimate being and destiny.

At this point I should like to suggest an approach which is quite the opposite. Secularization is *good*, it seems to me, insofar as it undermines excessive confidence in the religious instinct or intuition (Bonhoeffer calls it the "religious *a priori*"). The religious instinct appears to be a fairly universal phenomenon. Men have from time immemorial experienced wonder, mystery, awe, and dread in the face of the inexplicable and uncontrollable forces of nature and of their own inner nature, and have hypostatized these experiences in the gods. But critics as diverse as Calvin, Marx, Julian Huxley, and Bultmann have recognized that to give these experiences absolute status and authority is to fall into ideology. Calvin labeled the religious instinct "the idol factory of the human heart." And Marx was hopeful that as man more fully mastered his environment and destiny, residual religious feelings would wither away. The religious ideology would no longer be necessary when its source in human feelings of finitude and limitation had been overcome by man's success in organizing his world. Marx may have been overly optimistic in his prediction. Nevertheless, insofar as Marxism exposes the products of the religious instinct as ideology, as one stage in man's development which is now being made irrelevant, thus undermining confidence in the absoluteness of the religious intuition, Marxism may be Christianity's secret ally in world history. Secularization is therefore good as it undermines man's confidence in the ultimacy of the religious intuition as *the* clue to the divine.

However, from the same standpoint, secularization would be *bad* insofar as it itself turns into an ideology, secular*ism*, which collapses reality into a self-contained monolith, so that there is no longer anything or anyone to call man out of identity with his world into responsibility for it.

Where the gods are identical with the world, man can have no independence from it either. The political scientist, Erik Voegelin, points out that modern technological secularism has, in effect, reversed the movement which took place in ancient Israel. That ancient movement was one in which man achieved independence from his world by being called out of his identity with the cosmos to assume a place of responsibility over it. He was called to this independence and responsibility by a God who was different from the world. Only where God remains distinct from the world is this kind of call possible. When this God dies, the cosmos is the only reality left; the process reverses, and man slips back into identity with his world, back into the pre-Judeo-Christian form of religion.[3] Yes, modern secularism remains "religious," but it is a religion of identity: one aspect, one dimension of the world, is exalted, is mythologized, represents the whole. And the new, technologically monolithic world has shown an amazing propensity to spawn mythological expressions by which to give itself identity (now that it has lost its relativity to a transcendent God), myths of race, class, nation, blood, etc. Man continues to attempt to create within his windowless world some kind of absolute, some dimension of ultimacy. All he seems to be able to bring forth, however, is more fanaticism, the clash of absolute with absolute, of ideology with ideology, always attaching what is left of the religious instinct to his creations and demanding obeisance.

Altizer is, of course, just as opposed to this kind of idolatrous absolutizing of the world as is any sensitive thinker today. I do not see, however, that he has any real basis of norm within his approach of identity for calling man out of identity. The Archimedean point of reference is missing, for God has no dialectical reality apart from us as well as in our midst, no reality apart from the world as well as in it. Therefore, there is no basis from which to create what I would call genuine historical existence, nor any way to call man to what seems to me the vital need of our age, the vocation of responsible technological existence. Strictly speaking, a "vocation" cannot be self-

given; one must be called to it. And where there is no one
to call, the understanding of life as vocation drops away.
This is precisely modern man's problem. He no longer has
a context within which to understand his life as responsible to anyone but himself.

What is needed, therefore, is not a collapsing of reality
into a monolith of immanence but rather the recovery of
a language by which man can be called out of identity
into responsibility. This I take to be the crucial task of
theology in our time.

But allow me to push this questioning of Altizer a bit
farther. What he understands to be the point of identity
with ultimate reality, namely, the awareness of the sacred,
the sensitivity to the Word incarnating itself in our flesh,
I would contend—with the Marxists—is in actuality simply our own aesthetic faculty, a sensitivity with which
everyone is endowed to a greater or lesser degree. Most
of us have experienced "finitude" and "ecstasy," which
seem to mark off the standard range of "religious" awareness. To be sure, these experiences are also found in the
"way of distinction," where they may accompany the
event of relation. However, to paraphrase Martin Buber,
while they may accompany the event they do not constitute it.[4] Our aesthetic sensitivities, important as they are
in experiencing life to the full, are a part of the world, a
part of creation. To exalt them, including the most purely
"religious" intuitions, to some kind of absolute status, or,
which is to do the same thing, to assume that they are
the means of access to the ultimate, is to be involved in
ideology.

My own inclination is to say that genuine historical
existence, understood as relation with the Other, is possible only when all ideologies, including religious ideologies, are called into question. From where I stand, therefore, it looks as if the "radical theology" represented by
Altizer is not radical enough. Its atheism is a soft atheism.

It disposes of the transcendent God, to be sure, but puts in his place something that looks very much like an aesthetic ideology to which is attached the label, "Christ is alive!" In comparison with this, the hard atheism of a Sartre or a Camus, who refuses to be drawn into ideology, is still somehow more attractive.

Summarizing the crux of our difference of theological approach: From Altizer's standpoint, the God I am advocating, the God who is *distinct* from man and the world, is a repressive figure who must be killed in order that the God who in Christ is identical with the world might emerge. From my viewpoint, what needs to die, or at least to be relativized, is absolute confidence in the religious intuition of man, which in this form I take to be a deifying of the aesthetic dimension of the creature. For only when our confidence in the ultimacy of our instinctive religiousness has effectively been challenged, can we begin to be sensitive to the God who is distinct from man, who calls us out of identity with our world into responsibility for it.

I have posed the issues as forcefully as possible not to deny the contribution of Thomas Altizer but to affirm it. More than any of his colleagues in the theological movement of which he is a part, he is blazing new trails beyond the provincialism of Western theology. Even if one cannot agree with the particular amalgam of East and West which he is evolving, one cannot deny the importance of the task to which he has committed himself nor its usefulness as a stimulus to the overall task of arriving at a new language—or languages—which can communicate to man once again both divine and fully human existence, the goal we are all seeking.

NOTES

1. Gerhard Kruger, "Die Geschichte im Denken der Gegenwart," *Grosse Geschichtsdenker,* ed. by Rudolf Stadelmann (Tübingen, 1949), p. 224.

2. John H. Leith, ed., *Creeds of the Churches* (Doubleday & Company, Inc., 1963), p. 36.

3. Cf. Erik Voegelin, *Order and History,* Vol. I: *Israel and Revelation* (Louisiana State University Press, 1956).

4. Martin Buber, *I and Thou* (Charles Scribner's Sons, 1958), p. 14.

Harmon R. Holcomb

CHRISTOLOGY WITHOUT GOD:
A CRITICAL REVIEW OF
THE SECULAR MEANING OF THE GOSPEL

THE CONSIDERABLE EXCITEMENT among theologians and seminarians produced by Paul M. van Buren's *The Secular Meaning of the Gospel*[1] is deserved, not because the book is good, but because it has a certain importance. Poorly conceived, badly argued, and with an atrocious parade of scraps from analytical philosophy, the book is nevertheless both more interesting and more profitable than most essays in recent theology. As one of the young theologians who begin their theology with the "death of God," van Buren is refreshing because he really means it. Of the several current versions of the "death of God," his is the most radical and the clearest. Moreover, he is an intelligent writer struggling for clarity on the very issues which anyone who thinks theologically must face today.[2] To read the book carefully and to argue with its author is to gain light on the issues and some new knowledge of oneself. I count this a compliment, and if my assessment seems unduly harsh, I hasten now to urge the reader to secure the book and examine it carefully to his own profit.

Only the barest outline of the book's structure will be

From *Foundations*, January, 1965. Used by permission.

given here before we center attention upon its main thesis. The author sets his problem as the meaningless-ness of the language of the gospel today. The two alter-natives offered us in Karl Barth and Rudolf Bultmann are not helpful: Barth is true to Biblical language but asks us to forfeit our involvement in the modern world; Bultmann accepts our own historicity but loses the his-torical basis of the faith. Dietrich Bonhoeffer's suggestion of a "religionless Christianity" allows us to be the secular men we are, but it does not make meaningless Christian language meaningful. Either we make "being a Christian" an escape into some arcane realm of "the religious," or we must accept our faith as a human posture intelligible to men who are part of a secular culture. Taking our clues from analytical philosophy, we can learn how to accept the latter alternative and yet interpret the lan-guage of faith meaningfully.

A sympathetic interpretation of the Council of Chalce-don and the kind of Biblical theology to which it gave rise follows, but its Christology is rejected as "sadly mythological in form if not in content." Turning to the "left," the author tellingly criticizes Bultmann and Shu-bert Ogden for losing the historical Jesus, for wrongly interpreting New Testament language about events as language about human decisions, and for assuming the meaninglessness of the term "God." The development of van Buren's own position, which is our concern, is the heart of the remainder of the book.

Coming to the substance of the book, I must in fairness confess that I approach it with bias. The reader will be sufficiently warned when I add that I have found my bias comfortably and patly confirmed. The bias is not in favor of those obscurantist flights into safe "religious" realms, which van Buren fears as the great temptation. I simply find it prima facie implausible—even incoherent —to attempt the following tasks simultaneously: (1) to

make modern man's distrust of anything beyond himself
the unargued ground for reconstructing theology; (2) to
take as a tool for interpreting Christian language a
principle consonant with this distrust, alien to the Bible
and first devised to reflect the procedures of the natural
sciences; (3) to make the elimination of "God" a necessary condition for interpreting Christian theology meaningfully; (4) to regard Jesus as our "norm" only in the
elliptical sense of "Jesus Christ, properly reinterpreted by
the preceding principles"; and then (5) to claim that
in all of this you are being entirely faithful to the intent
of the New Testament and the church fathers.

Each point causes wonder, but taken together they produce a strong suspicion of incoherence. Why should
theology, of all things, be based on modern man's deliver-
ances about himself? Is not a Christology which dis-
penses with the God of the Bible a contradiction in
terms? If Scripture can no longer be the "Word of God,"
by definition, what is the sense of talking about being
faithful to Scripture?

One feels as one might upon hearing a man say, "I
shall now accomplish a task whose description is self-
contradictory." We would know ahead of time that he
could not know what his task was or what accomplish-
ing it would be, much less accomplish it. But to this kind
of initial doubt van Buren has an attractive counter. In
effect, he seems to say: "Wait and see. You are a modern
man informed by a secular culture, and my Christology
may find a response deep in you. You, too, are unsure of
God, bored with sermons, uneasy with the sacraments
and have little confidence or joy in the church." Since
this is too often true of most of us, we can do no less than
suspend our doubts for the while and accept his invitation to a secular pilgrimage through the New Testament
and theology. However, remembering that the journey
to which we are invited is described in self-contradictory

terms, we reserve the right to watch our guide carefully in order to see whether he has indeed found the Way or is himself the victim of a not-so-grand illusion.

I. THE BASIC FRAMEWORK: SECULARISM

The defining mark of modern man is secularism, a set of empirical attitudes expressing deep concern for everything human and a corresponding lack of interest in anything "beyond" this world. A secular man draws his models of understanding entirely from human experience and rejects any search for a religious realm or special religious way of knowing. All statements about God are to be interpreted as statements about men, and we must dispense with the meaningless word "God."

This assumption is unargued and functions as an axiom for van Buren's thesis. The reader may be saved some pointless counterargument by remembering this. The author does not use secularism as a neutral, factual description of our world, and grants that he does not know how widespread these secular attitudes are. Nor does he argue that his assumption is better or truer than that of traditional Christianity. He is making a proposal and an invitation. His secularism is offered normatively as a persuasive definition which is as nonarguable and nonprovable as Christian theism. It is, thus, his "blik," and there is no arguing about "bliks."[3]

This way of putting the basic assumption is the author's soft line and accounts for the repeated "I am only proposing, . . . inviting, . . . sharing. . . ." But, of course, he *does* argue as well; he *does* say that Biblical statements about God are meaningless as factual assertions, and he *does* claim a factual ground for his own position. There is no contradiction here. The soft line comes when he is proposing and describing his basic assumption, and the hard line comes when he is arguing from within that assumption and applying it. Fair enough, except that he frequently forgets and uses terms like "fact," "evidence," and "meaningful" as if they were neutral concepts, on the basis of which God is eliminated and secularism shown to be superior. Part of the apparent, but undeserved force of the book comes from this confusion, which obscures the fact that one faith is being proposed in place of another. Lovers of irony, however, will not begrudge it if a book advocating clarity profits from its own lack of it.

II. THE PRINCIPLE OF REINTERPRETATION: VERIFICATION

The purpose of the book is to answer the question, "How can a Christian who is himself a secular man understand his faith in a secular way?" The gospel is to be reinterpreted to meet this condition.

According to van Buren, the one hermeneutical principle consistent with our technological society is linguistic analysis based on the verification principle. "Statements of faith are to be interpreted, by means of the modified verification principle, as statements which express, describe, or commend a particular way of seeing the world, other men, and oneself, and the way of life appropriate to such a perspective."[4] What, then, is this central principle? Unfortunately, the author is anything but precise here and utilizes at least five versions without realizing that they have different consequences. There is no space here to document this charge, but two persistent confusions which vitiate his handling of the subject may be summarized: (a) confusion of "meaning-use in a language," with "meaning-verifiable by empirical standards"; and (b) confusion of the meaning of a term in *its* original context, with the meaning of a term in a preferred, reconstructed (van Buren's) context.

More important, the harrowing history of the principle of verification gives good reason to think that van Buren should not have used it at all. Briefly—and with violence to so complex a history—we can divide analytical philosophers into two poles and state the conclusions of each about the verification principle.

From the 1930's on, Ludwig Wittgenstein abjured the search for any *general* criterion by which authentic assertions could be demarcated from inauthentic ones. The men influenced by Wittgenstein held from the 1940's on that to ask for general criteria of meaningfulness was to ask a logically improper and futile question. Typical was John Wisdom's gibe that A. J. Ayer's revised version of the verification principle came to no more than: "Unless a statement has the sort of verification a scientific or commonsense statement has, it won't be a commonsense or scientific statement." When the verification principle is seen for what it is, "the poor thing is not what it was and is quite incapable of eliminating metaphysics or anything else." This theme has been common at Oxford right up through Gilbert Ryle's recent declaration that neither Wittgenstein nor anyone else has ever produced a criterion for detecting authentically referring expressions. In short, one pole of analytical philosophy gives no support to van Buren's use of the verification principle as a criterion of cognitive significance. One of the puzzling things about the book is the author's sincere tribute to the influence of Wittgenstein, coupled with his total failure to use Wittgenstein's methods of analysis.

Van Buren's practice has more in common with the second, or reconstructionist pole of analytical philosophy. A long-sought goal has been to eliminate all nonempirical terms (other than logical terms) from the natural sciences and to reconstruct the language so that every term will be an experiential term or related to these by stateable inferences. There is some structural similarity here to van Buren's goal of eliminating nonempirical terms like "God" and of reconstructing the Christian language so that the perspective expressed by it will have an empirical base.

The history of the philosophers' search is instructive, but only the conclusion to it can be given here. From the outset, the trouble was that any criterion of verifiability strong enough to eliminate terms like "God" or "soul" or "vital force" was too strong to allow the retention of certain terms which the sciences need and happily use. Theoretical terms like "electron" or "positron" are non-observational, and the verification principle was successively weakened to accommodate them, but to no avail. Today it is generally held, as Carl Hempel says, that no scientific theory can be translated into either a finite or infinite class of empirical statements, and the nonempirical terms can have their meaning only partly specified.[5] Scheffler puts the moral: "For we have traveled a long way from the conception of empiricism as a shiny, new philosophical doctrine for weeding out obscurantism and nonsense wherever they crop up; . . . [and] even a modest empiricism is presently a hope for clarification, rather than a well-grounded doctrine, unless we construe it in a quite trivial way."[6] Van Buren writes like a man who has just discovered that shiny, new doctrine, and he does construe it in a quite trivial way.

The verification principle is absolutely essential to the whole of the book, as the author says, but his confidence in it is misplaced. He uses a standard of cognitive meaningfulness which the natural sciences cannot meet, and surely this is irresponsible on the part of an empiricist. But still, it might be objected, "God" and "electron" function in vastly different ways in statements, and the former is completely incapable of empirical testing. Of course, but what is to the point here may be phrased as a challenge: before anyone rules out theological statements as cognitively meaningless, let him state his criterion. When this is produced, very good reasons can be given for holding (*a*) that no such general criterion is logically proper or fruitful, and (*b*) that any such criterion would rule out some things an empiricist has to defend as well as what he wants to reject. Van Buren's basic principle of interpretation rests on a self-defeating proposal.

From his failure to discuss the problems involved, one gathers that van Buren regards the notion of "what would count for or against an assertion" as an intuitively clear notion. Most of the time it is clear enough, but the celebrated "paradoxes of confirmation" should make us cautious about our intuitions. By appealing to intuitively clear principles which we all use, "All ravens are black" turns out to be confirmed by any object whatsoever (e.g., a blue pencil or a yellow bonnet), a result which makes the "confirmation" ridiculous. There is every prospect that paradoxes like this can be resolved, but their presence shows that there is no intuitively clear meaning to "what counts for, or confirms" such that one can simply appeal to it.

III. The Reconstruction of the Gospel

Application of the verification principle to Christian language results in the discovery of what van Buren regards as the true function of the language: (*a*) it is cognitively meaningless if taken (mistakenly) to be a series of propositions capable of truth or falsity; (*b*) it is not a series of assertions about God and his acts, cosmology, or the like; (*c*) it is meaningful as the expression of the basic attitudes of one who has been caught by the historical perspective which has Jesus at its center; (*d*) its meaningful reference is to the Christian way of life; and (*e*) it often functions simply to enlighten the listener concerning the believer's "blik," or to invite others to share that "blik."[7]

If the methodological key to this book is the verification principle, the substance of the book comes from the application of the principle to the historical Jesus. Van Buren adopts Collingwood's version of historical knowledge, and then expresses a robust confidence in the ability of the New Quest scholars (e.g., Bornkamm, Fuchs, Ebeling, Robinson) to deliver to us enough of the historical Jesus for a secular Christology. This is strange on two counts: first, the redefinition of "history" at the hands of the men mentioned is anathema to most empiricists, under whose banner van Buren has enrolled; and second, the whole New Quest enterprise is rooted in philosophical and theological commitments which van Buren does not share and which are too shaky to deserve the confident use he makes of them. Amazingly, he devotes only a few pages to the whole nest of problems concerning the recovery of the historical Jesus, even though this is essential. "Faith is not based simply on a picture of the historical Jesus, but the historical Jesus is indispensable for faith."[8] The sentiment is admirable, but the reader must remember that here the historical Jesus means the Jesus recovered by the methods of the New Quest, and reinterpreted via the verification principle. To the extent that the reader has doubts about these methods, his doubt infects van Buren's second main principle.

Only one case in point will be mentioned. Van Buren *defines* Jesus by his freedom and illustrates as follows:

> He was free from anxiety and the need to establish his own identity, but he was above all free for his neighbor. . . . He was, apparently, a man free to give himself to others, whoever they were. He lived thus, and he was put to death for being this kind of man in the midst of fearful and defensive men.[9]

Now, to know these things would be to know a great deal about the inner life of Jesus, his feelings as he faced death, and the inner motives of those who killed him. Rudolf Bultmann has reminded his New Quest descendants that we do not know any of these things to be true on the basis of historical research. Bultmann claims that *qua* empirical historians, we do not know the motives of Jesus in going to Jerusalem, the inner attitudes with which he faced death, or the meaning he placed on his own death. Empirically, we would need an almost impossible amount of evidence before declaring of a contemporary, "He is free of anxiety." The Gospels are not concerned with that kind of evidence nor with the question that prompts the demand for it.

It will not do to reply that the picture in the gospel is of a totally free person, and that it is this picture which becomes the believer's norm. Van Buren often takes this way out, but it will not do because *somewhere* there has to be an empirically warranted ground for his own reconstruction of the gospel. Otherwise, references to Jesus are wholly of the order of "bliks," and his reconstruction is then, on his own terms, as unempirical as Christian theology.

Is the question whether Jesus was wholly free an empirically decidable question or not? Clearly it is not. It is, however, an empirically meaningful question even if, because of the time lapse, its truth or falsity can never be decided. Van Buren simply assumes that "Jesus was free . . ." is in fact true, and gets more from his empirical base than he is entitled to. Had he begun all his sentences with "If Jesus was in fact free, then . . . ," or "There being some probability that Jesus was free, we can surmise . . . ," the secular meaning of the gospel would have had a different tone.

Turning now to the application of the verification principle to the Gospels, let us look at some examples of the reconstructions of meaning which result.

a. "He trusted in the God of love" has the cash value of "He loved men" and "He was willing to die."[10]

b. "He is risen" means that on Easter the freedom of Jesus began to be "contagious," and the disciples discerned Jesus in a new way and began to share the freedom which had been his.[11]

c. "In saying that *God* raised up Jesus, the disciples indicated that what had happened to them was fundamental to their life and thought: Jesus as the liberator had become the point from which they saw the world and lived in it."[12]

d. "In telling the story of Jesus of Nazareth, . . . they told it as the story of the free man who had set them free. This was the story which they proclaimed as the Gospel for all men."[13]

e. "He died for our sins" means that Jesus' death was "regarded as the measure of the freedom for which he set other men free."[14]

f. "He died for the sins of the whole world" means that he was "free for every man, those who did not acknowledge him as well as those that did."[15]

g. "Jesus was sinless" means that Jesus was free, and he defines freedom for me and furnishes the norm by which others are in bondage.[16]

h. "The eternal Son, without ceasing to be God, became flesh" means that, as one caught by the contagion of Jesus, I, like all lovers, use extended language and "final" words about the one who defines my perspective.[17]

And so on. This, then, is "the secular meaning of the gospel," and when we tell the old, old story we are defining, expressing, and commending a certain historical perspective. This assertion is itself a recommendation by van Buren to modern man to salvage what is valuable in the gospel by seeing it in this light.

IV. THE RECONSTRUCTION CONSIDERED:
THE PROBLEM OF "TRANSLATION"

Most of us would acknowledge that the problem which van Buren is facing is a fundamental one for us. The question now is: Has he provided a helpful answer? For him the problem occurs in its most acute form because he is claiming three things simultaneously: (*a*) to eliminate reference to God; (*b*) to provide a humanistic language which is "functionally equivalent" to the New Testament and the fathers; and (*c*) to remain fully faithful to their intent. As before, this looks impossible. Does he bring it off?

A glance at the reconstructions in the preceding section will reveal a monotony in his reinterpretations. The pattern is the same, no matter what New Testament sentence is being "analyzed": the freedom of Jesus, contagion, my perspective. The richness of the New Testament is lost by the wooden application of a schema, and van Buren finds a unity in its writings undreamed of by the most orthodox scholars. Not even the many tools of linguistic philosophy are used. It is as if a blind man with a meat cleaver were essaying delicate surgery: the patient is not likely to be the same afterward; similarly, any equivalence of meaning discerned will be the result of drastic plastic surgery.

A second glance at the list of reinterpretations supports our observation that Wittgenstein's slogan, "The meaning of a sentence is its use in the language," is praised but ignored. Van Buren does not analyze New Testament language in its own context; he is interested in extracting what is acceptable *after* the Scripture has been pruned by a standard congenial to a modern humanist. Hence, there can be no question of *identity* of meaning or function in the original context with that in the preferred, reduced context. True, our author claims not identity but functional equivalence. It is evident that the emphasis is on "functional," but we have not yet located any "equivalence."

In order to claim any equivalence of meaning, van Buren has to resort to the Bultmannian distinction between form and intent, and assert, like Bultmann, that he can retain the intent without the form. If theological assertions are as logically odd as he describes them, his confidence that he can grasp their true intent is surprising. He is in the awkward position of having to hold that he knows the true intention of the Gospel writers, although they, being blinded by a meaningless belief system, were unable to state what they meant. But how could he know their hidden intent? We have no independent evidence. Furthermore, the verification principle is not a principle for getting at intentions; it is a device for locating sentences which are subject to observational tests, another matter altogether. In shifting to intentions, van Buren undermines his empiricism.

When van Buren was stressing the equivalence of statements on the basis of their cash value in experience, this was consonant with his use of the verification principle. Remember, "Jesus trusted in the God of Love" was said to have the cash value of "Jesus loved men and was willing to die." Now, needing an equivalence stronger than cash value so as to claim faithfulness to intent, van Buren shifts without noticing it. He has to shift because cash value equivalence is not the same as equivalence of intent. The cash value of "featherless biped" and "Homo sapiens" is the same, but their meanings are not equivalent. Or to take a hoary example, "morning star" and "evening star" both denote Venus and cash out the same in testing, but they do not mean the same. This is further complicated by belief contexts. "Thales believed that the morning star was divine" does not mean that he believed in the divinity of the evening star. Cash value equivalence is no index of equivalence of intent, especially in contexts of belief.

Some findings of Willard Quine are apropos here. After years of working at the reconstruction of language on the basis of nominalism, Quine has concluded that: (*a*) the *speaker* of a language is the final judge as to whether someone else's reconstruction satisfies his intent; (*b*) no language is intentionally isomorphic with its reconstruction; and (*c*) sentences which can be equated on the basis of behavioral responses are few in number and woefully underdetermine the hypotheses on which all further translation rests.

As for Quine's first finding, there is good evidence that the speakers of the New Testament would have regarded van Buren's reconstruction as a dangerous form of unbelief. Taken together, the other two propositions tell us that van Buren ought to give up either his empiricism or his claim to grasp hidden intentions. But either course is fatal to his position. Without his strange, nonempirical intentions there is no equivalence of intent, functional or otherwise; and without this there is no faithfulness to the real intent of the New Testament. But if he keeps his mastery of hidden intentions, he forsakes his axiom of empiricism, and then there was no point in starting the book.

V. THE PROBLEM OF REDUCTION

Van Buren is willing to reduce the New Testament to his preferred language because he believes that what is omitted does not matter. This leads to a startling principle of reinterpretation: "Fidelity to intention demands transformation of language"; and, "To clarify the function of the language of Chalcedonian Christology, precisely by being disloyal to its assertions, is to show that our interpretation is faithful to the Chalcedonian intent."[18] Disloyalty to the apparent intent is loyalty to the true intent!

This statement would make sense to me if the New Testament and Chalcedon had been conceived *originally* as allegories, or at least written to be read on two levels, like some writings of the underground during the Occupation. But there is no evidence that the New Testament and Chalcedon were trying to do anything except speak directly on what they took to be true, viz., God's revelation in Christ. If so, van Buren's reductive interpretations are bound to omit what mattered in the original writings. One example is the exegetical results obtained by his method. In interpreting "He who hath seen me hath seen the Father," he makes the apparent intent (The search for God is successfully completed because God shows himself in the Son) mean the same thing as the reinterpreted intent (The search should never have been started because there is no God to find).[19] To equate these two indicates that his principle of interpretation is as wrong as it is mysterious.

But, says the author, reductive programs are a familiar fact of modern history: astrology has been reduced to astronomy and alchemy to chemistry, and theology cannot escape this tendency. This assumes that ridding Christian belief of "God" is parallel to the relation between astronomy and astrology. Surely, if analogies are to be used, more appropriate ones would be ridding science of the concept of law, or logic of axioms, or biology of "organism," or physical theory of its basic but nonobservational terms. The consequences would be serious, to say the least.

VI. THE EMPIRICAL BASIS OF A SECULAR CHRISTOLOGY

Our author wants a Christology, but one which has an "empirical footing," for it would otherwise be unintelligible to secular man. We must ask now about this empirical basis, and the connections between it and the perspective it defines. The connections are important, because a system does not become empirical merely by having a historical person at its center. One can have all sorts of nonempirical beliefs about a man.

A Christology requires more than ethical language, so van Buren wants to preserve the force and finality of theological language. To do this he must accept "extended" language about Jesus, i.e., language extended beyond what is testable about, or appropriate to, a man. A believer, he says, is like a lover and naturally uses highly expressive language about the one who is the center of his life. Words of wonder, awe, and worship are natural when used of Jesus as the norm of one's perspective. If the believer understands that this extended use is expressive of his own attitude, then his "use of the language of praise and adoration is perfectly appropriate. God of God, Light of Light, very God of very God."[20]

The path from statements about the historical Jesus to adoring him as "God of God" is a long one filled with nonempirical leaps, but without this extended use of language van Buren could not offer his reconstruction as a Christology. Why is this extended usage acceptable, while that of the believer in God is meaningless?

As nearly as I can make out, van Buren has two answers to this. The first answer consists in saying that his extended language expresses a basic perspective. Does this help? No, because it equally helps the Christian defend his extended language about the God who was in Christ. If the extended language in both perspectives is unverifiable but essential, then they are on the same footing as far as the verification principle goes. Had van Buren applied the same standard to his Christological language that he did to theological language, the results would have been very similar. A ready reply to this criticism is that the cases are different: theological

statements try to say something true about an unverifiable God. But would van Buren want to deny that the
secular believer is trying to say something true about
Jesus Christ that is not verifiable about the historical
Jesus? He would not want to say that he really does *not*
mean it when he uses words of wonder, awe, and
worship, and that this is just the odd way he talks about
his perspective.

The second answer van Buren appears to give to the
question about his use of unverifiable language takes the
form of stressing the noncognitive, nonfactual, purely
expressive nature of his extended language about Jesus.
But, far from being an answer, this is what *constitutes*
the problem of giving the required empirical base. It
seems that the empirical language in his scheme refers
to the historical Jesus, while the extended language expresses one's attitudes. But does he mean one's attitudes
toward Jesus or one's attitudes toward the exalted Jesus
whom one worships and adores as norm of his life? This
is parallel to the old Jesus-of-history and Christ-of-faith
debate, and finding an empirical ground for the latter in
the former is much the same in both cases. The more he
stresses this approach, the more his position is indis-
tinguishable from those existentialist interpretations so
roundly criticized earlier in the book.

To have a Christology, van Buren has to have the
finality and religiously commanding force of worship and
adoration expressible only in extended language. This,
however, severs the connection with an empirically testable base and is incompatible with his basic principle.
The moral seems to be that you cannot have a Christology on the basis of a humanism. A humanist who likes
to use Christological language just muddies waters which
were never too clear.

This, the most forthright of the Christian writings
based on the "death of God," is a failure, but the failure

of an intelligent man of integrity who rightly desires clarity and truth. As such, it is more enlightening and profitable than most of the safer efforts. Still, his invitation to a Christian pilgrimage which begins with the death of God was an invitation to an impossible journey, and we should not overly praise the results. Modern literature is obsessed with death in all its forms, including the death of God. However, who and what is dead is a question not so easily settled as in this book.

NOTES

1. Paul M. van Buren, *The Secular Meaning of the Gospel* (The Macmillan Company, 1963).

2. For an appreciation of this, see the excellent review by Langdon Gilkey in *The Journal of Religion*, Vol. XLIV, No. 3 (July, 1964), pp. 238–243.

3. Van Buren, *op. cit.*, pp. 85, 155. The term "blik" is taken from R. M. Hare's essay in *New Essays in Philosophical Theology*, ed. by A. Flew and A. MacIntyre (London: SCM Press, Ltd., 1953), pp. 99–105. Van Buren follows Antony Flew in interpreting a "blik" as the expression of a basic attitude held independently of any factual assertions. In my opinion, this misconstrues Hare's intent. Hare interprets a "blik" as a nontestable *assertion* which makes possible the testing of other assertions. This is a rejection of Flew's assumption that if a statement is not empirically verifiable it has no assertable content, and, in fact, Hare grants cognitive significance to certain metaphysical and theological statements. With this demurrer, I shall adopt van Buren's version throughout this review.

4. Van Buren, *op. cit.*, p. 156.

5. See Carl G. Hempel, "The Theoretician's Dilemma," in *Minnesota Studies in the Philosophy of Science*, Vol. II, ed. by H. Feigel, M. Scriven, and G. Maxwell (University of Minnesota Press, 1958), pp. 37–98; and also Carl G. Hempel, "Operationism, Observation, and Theoretical Terms," in *Phil-*

osophy of Science, ed. by A. Danto and S. Morgenbesser (Meridian Books, 1960), pp. 101–120.

6. Israel Scheffler, "Theoretical Terms and a Modest Empiricism," in Danto and Morgenbesser, *op cit.,* pp. 172–173. A more extensive treatment is given in Israel Scheffler, *The Anatomy of Inquiry* (Alfred A. Knopf, Inc., 1963), pp. 127–226. Flew actually uses falsifiability as a criterion of significance, and van Buren adopts this and confuses it with a principle of verifiability, but I have not exploited this since it does not matter in the end. See Scheffler, *op. cit.,* pp. 137–149.

7. Van Buren, *op. cit.,* pp. 99–101.

8. *Ibid.,* p. 126.

9. *Ibid.,* p. 123.

10. *Ibid.*

11. *Ibid.,* pp. 132 f.

12. *Ibid.,* p. 133.

13. *Ibid.,* p. 134.

14. *Ibid.,* p. 151.

15. *Ibid.,* p. 152.

16. *Ibid.,* pp. 163 f.

17. *Ibid.,* pp. 161–163, 169.

18. *Ibid.,* pp. 158 f.

19. *Ibid.,* pp. 146 f.

20. *Ibid.,* p. 162.

Julian Hartt

IS CHRISTIANITY FINISHED?
A REVIEW OF GABRIEL VAHANIAN'S
THE DEATH OF GOD

M R. VAHANIAN is concerned to show how contemporary life is governed by assumptions no longer Christian even in vague profession. He seeks to show how other forms of religiousness, other "gods," have arisen, and notably the exaltation of man himself to the position once enjoyed by Christ alone. "In Toynbee's warning, the danger today is not a re-emergence of nature-worship but the creeping religiosity of man-worship." This is a religiousness which carries with it an anthropocentric ethic (what Szczesny applauds, Vahanian decries). But Vahanian attempts to give his analysis an empirical grounding: "God's absence, or the death of God itself, has become what a man directly experiences."

At the risk of appearing either dull-witted or callous to the spiritual misery of contemporary man, we have to ask, Who is this man to whom God's absence is an item of direct and immediate experience? Heidegger speaks of the silence of God in our time; and a host of lesser figures in the café world chant the refrain; but here, surely, each man must speak for himself and keep silence for himself. I suppose, therefore, that what Vahanian

From *The Nation*, September 30, 1961. Used by permission.

means by the "death of God" is the relative poverty of belief in the God of traditional Christian affirmation. But here his essay suffers cruelly from deficient analysis. He does not know how many people still believe in that God, nor does anybody else know. He does not know how many people think ill of their moral performance because they cannot square it with their belief in God. Then what evidence is available in support of the cry that "God is dead"? There is the testimony of creative artists who, by definition, reveal the ethos, and the all-pervading sense in our culture that the transcendent dimensions of existence are lost to view. But here again we have to ask how Vahanian knows this sense has gone so far and done so much damage. We intellectuals seem to know all about this; but our confidence touches the earth of fact very gingerly indeed.

What puzzles me about Vahanian's views here is his strong argument in support of his thesis that there never was a Christian civilization. His attack on Eliot, for instance, is brisk and persuasive. Moreover, his criticisms of Maritain's Catholic humanism are shrewd and perhaps march to the triumph of proving that a Christian civilization is an impossible (and, just possibly, sinful) dream anyway. Very well. But then why and how speak of "post-Christian"? I suppose he means to show that the Christian faith no longer serves as the inevitable and productive ground for criticism of culture. Men have always done immoral and foolish things, no doubt; but now they no longer judge these things to be either immoral or foolish by Christian standards: that is, the generality does not do so. And this because immanental religiousness has replaced every authentic sense of the transcendent.

I have already expressed my conviction that Vahanian does not in fact know this much about the generality of existing persons. There are two further problems: one, he should have learned from his existentialistic mentors, beginning with Kierkegaard, that the decisive moment of "faith" is inalienably solitary. What, in his solitariness, a person really believes, and what he really loves and is prepared to entrust with his soul's treasure, may have very inadequate external registration. Today we incline strongly to view this situation as abnormal, and persistence in maintaining it, a vice. But because the forces making for uniformity of attitude and opinion are so strong, the resistant inner life becomes more heavily disguised; and the normalities of commerce with the external world become less and less reliable as indices of that inner condition.

And the second problem: if we have indeed entered the post-Christian religious age, the vestigial Christian—theologian and other—has an impossible assignment, really impossible, for then the ground and principle of his critique of this age are meaningless; and his persistence in criticism must by his contemporaries be judged to be an exercise in obsolete piety and by himself a duty rendered only to God experienced as a nullity or an absence.

So here again Vahanian is in something like the situation of Szczesny. Ostensibly, he is reporting the spiritual actualities of the present age. Actually, he is making a series of theological judgments upon these actualities. Unless his procedure is purely confessional, he has an obligation therefore to support that theological ground of criticism; and thereafter to show how ethical prescriptions are entailed by a true theology.

Vahanian is right in saying that the "spirit of the age" is immanental. It is in fact introspective, to a horrid fault. And somehow, it is thought, the full and proper expression of our plight will open a door to truth and grace. Which being translated means that even theologians are capable of confusing the psychological difficulties people profess to have in believing something with the degree of intelligibility that thing may in itself have or may want. Hence . . . if Vahanian is convinced that the Biblical faith is true, let him stand on it and not worry whether one who so believes is bound to cut a sorry figure among the enlightened. There is a time to mourn the misery of the present age but it is not the same time as that in which a man either makes his own witness or confesses his own emptiness a defect rather than a virtue. It happens that at the present moment the spokesmen of religious emptiness include more prizewinners in the arts than the ranks of piety can boast. So what? Are the former the only "authentic" spirits above ground? So to believe is presumption or parochialism, or something compact of both.

F. Thomas Trotter

VARIATIONS
ON THE "DEATH OF GOD" THEME
IN RECENT THEOLOGY

THE EXPRESSION the "death of God" is now well established in the theological vocabulary. Widespread use in publication points to the popularity if not the precise definition of the term. Bishop John A. T. Robinson's *Honest to God*[1] has brought the theme into the busy pastor's study and even into the mass-media periodicals. As an expression, the "death of God" is very much alive.

In a time of widespread "religiosity," the possibility of serious discussion of the theme is hampered by lack of precision in definition. One observes both panic in the face of "atheism" on the part of defenders of orthodoxy, and uncritical enthusiasm for the expression on the part of dilettanti. Forensic alarms from the former and superficial slogans from the latter serve only to obscure the truly serious issues in the new situation in theology.

The variations on the theme of the "death of God"—absence, disappearance, silence, withdrawal, eclipse—indicate the particular character of the theological problem but also reveal the difficulty in defining exactly what the

From *The Journal of Bible and Religion*, January, 1965. Copyright © by American Academy of Religion, 1965. Used by permission.

Nietzschean expression means in contemporary theological vocabulary. This article will note briefly the historical situation which produced the expression, then indicate three basic variations on the theme in Sartre, Heidegger, and Buber, and finally illustrate how five young American theologians—Vahanian, Altizer, Hamilton, van Buren, and Cobb—deal with the expression.

I

The striking—and problematic—shape of the term belongs, of course, to Nietzsche, who gave extended expression to the phrase. Contemporary usage is certainly attributable to him, although Buber notes that the term had been employed by Hegel as early as 1802.[2] The content of the "death of God" expression, however, is the religious and philosophical heritage of three hundred years of Western thought from Copernicus to Nietzsche. This period saw the great confessional debates, the rise of rationalism and pietism, and the general erosion of classical doctrinal theology. It has been suggested that Western thought had engaged itself since the seventeenth century in either "outflanking" or "attacking" God.[3] The former mood reached its fullest expression in the French Encyclopedists, while the latter found its final shape in Nietzsche.

The debate accelerated and reached its climax in the nineteenth century. The rationalistic atheism of the eighteenth century became the polemical atheism of the nineteenth. Kierkegaard ("faith as subjectivity"), Dostoevsky ("faith as unbelief"), Feuerbach ("faith as appetite"), and Strauss ("faith as obsolete") all experimented with theological atheism. Melville in America, Browning in England, and Baudelaire in France explored facets of the "death of God" in literary form. J. Hillis Miller, in a useful study, has identified five responses to the theme in the nineteenth-century literature: humanism, perspectivism, nihilism, pious acceptance, and romanticism.[4] The pervasiveness of the problem of unbelief in the nineteenth century is illustrated by Margaret Maison in her study of Victorian religion. "Never has any age in history produced such a detailed literature of lost faith, or so many great men and women of religious temperament standing outside organized religion."[5] Miss Maison is of the opinion that it would be instructive to compile a list of eminent Victorians who lost their faith in the fray, and she does offer a list of those who were destined for careers in the church but renounced them. The list includes Carlyle, Clough, Ruskin, Pater, Hardy, Burne-Jones, Tennyson, Froude, and even Darwin.[6]

Surveying nineteenth-century literature from the vantage point of the mid-twentieth century, one wonders how this inexorable erosion of faith could have progressed so far without widespread notice. Carl Becker, in a fortunate metaphor, suggests that "it was as if a rumor, started no one knew when, had at last become too insistent to be longer disregarded: the rumor that God, having departed secretly in the night, was about to cross the frontiers of the known world and leave mankind in the lurch. What we have to realize is that in those years God was on trial."[7]

If God was on trial, it was Nietzsche who announced that sentence had been passed. "God is dead. God remains dead. And we have killed him. How shall we, the murderers of all murderers, comfort ourselves? What was holiest and most powerful of all that the world has yet owned has bled to death under our knives."[8] This announcement gave vividness to the spiritual crisis of Western thought. The issue was the erosion and bankruptcy of religious sensitivity. Among Nietzsche's powerful images is that of the old saint digging for roots in the forest while Zarathustra brings down fire from the mountain. "Can it be possible? This old Saint in his forest has not yet heard the news that *God is dead?*"

Kirillov, in *The Possessed,* suggests that history may be divided into two periods: from the gorilla to the annihilation of God and from the annihilation of God to the transformation of man.[9] Like Dostoevsky, whose heroes sought a new man-Godhood, Nietzsche also proclaimed a new anthropology. With the death of God, Nietzsche announced that man was freed from superstition and the bonds of slavery to divine tyranny, and would now be able to find joyful release in his human fulfillment. God is an otiose hypothesis, as Laplace was reported to have explained to Napoleon. God's place will remain empty, man will not be God, but he will be Superman: "Can you create a god?—Then be silent about all gods! But you could create the Superman. Perhaps you yourselves cannot, my brothers! But you can recreate yourselves to be the fathers and forefathers of the Superman: let that be your best creation!"[10] The Nietzschean proclamation is primarily an announcement of the death of metaphysics or the death of revelation. The superman functions out of the subjective rather than the suprasensory realm of divine existence. What has died is the "reality" of an order of existence that is "other" than self-perception and subjective appropriation. A new anthropology is the only possible positive response to the collapse of metaphysics. As Langan notes, "the divine *fiat* has given place to a new scepter wielded by man: *die Technik.*"[11]

Martin Buber, summarizing the impact of Nietzsche, notes that the "death of God" means "only that man has become incapable of apprehending a reality absolutely independent of himself and of having a relation with it— incapable, moreover, of imaginatively perceiving this reality and representing it in images, since it eludes direct contemplation."[12] As such, the crisis of faith in Western culture is indeed deep and decisive for faith. Philosophy, theology, and the arts in our time remain Nietzschean in this sense. The problem is one of "digging out of the Nietzschean ruins," as William Barrett has suggested.[13]

II

To "fill the horizon that has been declared empty" is the way Buber has defined the task of philosophy and religion since Nietzsche. Three post-Nietzschean proposals may be viewed as major types of "death of God" exposition. The theme may be illustrated by Jean-Paul Sartre ("God is dead"), Martin Heidegger ("God is absent"), and Martin Buber ("God is in eclipse"). Each illustrates an emphasis latent in Nietzsche but in a manner somewhat different from the nuances of the others. Together they illustrate the fact that unity in definition of the term "death of God" is quite problematic.

a. "God is dead." Sartre describes his system as an "attempt to draw all the consequences of a coherent atheistic position." The proclamation is to be understood literally. In fact Sartre, in a rather crude phrase, has suggested that God "spoke to us and now is silent, all that we touch now is his corpse."[14] It may be distressing that God does not exist, because all possibility of finding values in a heaven of ideas disappears along with God. "Nausea," the vivid symbol of anxiety in the face of awareness of the collapse of value structures, takes the place of joy and delight in contemplation of God. With the "death of God," no longer are there metaphysical or theological supports for moral action. Man is thrust into his selfhood and loneliness to act responsibly—to be, in short, a man.

b. "God is absent." Heidegger rejects the "coherent atheism" of Sartre and remarks that his own thought "can no more be theistic than it can be atheistic."[15] The "death of God" for Heidegger is awareness of God's absence from the world. The question of the possibility of God is simply no longer posed for man. Unlike Sartre, for whom the existence of God is a matter of indifference, Heidegger argues from the limitations of human thought. He has demonstrated his profound respect for the problem of God by insisting that our traditional conceptual tools are inadequate for the theological task. He turns to the poet Hölderlin for insight and may be himself identified with the position he attributes to the poet who stands "in the no-more of the departed gods and the not-yet of the coming" God.[16]

James M. Robinson and John B. Cobb, Jr., have introduced the notion of the "later Heidegger" in a way which suggests that the philosopher is moving in the direction of a more articulate theistic position. But this movement is based fundamentally upon the assumption that theology needs a more adequate category than metaphysics. To that extent, Heidegger shares with Sartre the general existentialist posture.

c. "God is in eclipse." Martin Buber shows some affinities with Heidegger's emphases, particularly in his agreeing that man must practice "openness" and "readiness" to Being. He rejects the notion that one can adequately account for the nihilistic character of our time by observing the changes that have taken place in man's spirit. He also counters Heidegger's skepticism regarding the "suprasensory" world. God is not dead in the literal sense as in Sartre, nor is he absent merely because conceptual tools are inadequate or corroded as in Heidegger. Man cannot unveil the mystery but rather he must admit himself to "the effective reality of transcendence as such." An eclipse, Buber reminds us, is something that occurs between the sun and our eyes, not in the sun itself.[17] For Buber, the "death of God" is an unfortunate phrase, "eclipse" being a more adequate term. However, he agrees with Sartre and Heidegger in the recognition of a "religious need" in modern man. Buber argues that the problem is much deeper than one of dismissing "religious" needs; it lies in the possibility that something is inherent in human existence which cannot be dismissed. The response of Buber is to shift the Sartrian "subject-object" dialectic to the Biblical "I-Thou" relation:

> God can never become an object for me; I can attain no other relation to Him than that of the I to its eternal Thou, that of the Thou to its eternal I. But if man is no longer able to attain this relation, if God is silent toward him and he toward God, then something has taken place, not in human subjectivity but in Being itself. It would be worthier not to explain it to oneself in sensational and incompetent sayings, such as that of the "death" of God, but to endure it as it is and at the same time to move existentially toward a new happening, toward that event in which the word between heaven and earth will again be heard.[18]

III

The impact of the "death of God" philosophy upon twentieth-century literature does not need extensive elaboration. Rainer Maria Rilke, probably the most consistent "Nietzschean" poet, echoes the theme throughout his work. "God is the no longer sayable," writes Rilke, "and his attributes fly back into his Creation." Franz Kafka, Albert Camus, Graham Greene, Marcel Proust, André Gide, William Faulkner, Thomas Mann—all witness to a world in which God is "silent," "absent," "disappeared," or "dead." The attraction of the theme to the novelist is one of the striking features of the whole movement. It is the mood of the time, the spiritual malaise of the culture, that the most vivid experience of God's absence is apparent.

In this "new situation" have appeared a number of thoughtful works by younger theologians. By and large, these scholars are students of scholars who themselves sought to frame their work within the context of the new cultural situation: Barth, Tillich, Bultmann, Bonhoeffer, Eliade, and Whitehead. Each of the younger scholars, while indebted to the previous generation, represents new and sometimes radical directions. The following are representative of the varieties of recent post-Nietzschean theologizing. Although they certainly do not exhaust the list of outstanding younger theological writers, they represent five fairly distinct reactions to the new situation in theology.

a. *The New Iconoclasm.* Gabriel Vahanian, whose *Death of God: The Culture of Our Post-Christian Era*[19] is an attempt to give systematic expression to the "death of God" idea in contemporary culture, attacks the "idols" of religiosity. "To speak of the death of God means . . . that finally at the end of the Christian phase of Western culture, the reality of the living God is freed from the cultural concepts and other institutions which attempt to objectify and domesticate it. The death of God marks the end of Christian culture and, especially, of its attempt to assimilate *the other God,* the living God of whom our religion as well as our diffuse religiosity is a desperate caricature."[20] Vahanian is an iconoclast in the same sense that Kierkegaard and Nietzsche were attackers of the complacency of the church. Like his mentor, Karl Barth, Vahanian attacks "religiosity," "existentialism," and "immanentalism" and proposes restoration of the Barthian accent upon transcendence.

b. *The New Immanentalism.* Thomas J. J. Altizer is a student of Joachim Wach and Mircea Eliade, the great historians of religion. Altizer emphasizes the dialectical accents of Nietzsche's doctrine of Eternal Recurrence. The proclamation of the "death of God" is also the announcement of the possibility of human existence. "A No-Saying to God (the transcendence of *Sein*) makes possible a Yes-Saying to human existence (*Dasein*, total existence in the *here* and *now*). Absolute transcendence is transformed into absolute immanence."[21] Altizer calls for a "genuinely dialectic" theology that refuses to be gnostic because of its affirmation of the present and likewise refuses to be dogmatic because of its negation of the nondialectical past. "If theology is to transcend itself it must negate itself, for theology can be reborn only through the death of Christendom, which finally means the death of the Christian God, the God who is the transcendence of Being."[22] Altizer argues that Christendom understood the incarnation as a nondialectical (or partial) union of flesh and spirit, time and eternity. The result was an autonomous history. This inevitably led to the "death of God" understood as the willing transformation of the sacred into the profane, the nondialectical separation of man from meaningful existence. The problem for theology, then, is the recovery of a truly dialectical faith in which the sacred and the profane are not separated and in which authentic existence is possible.

c. *The New Ethics.* William Hamilton's debt to Dietrich Bonhoeffer is evident throughout his work. His is a "world come of age" and he takes as his theological task to speak to thoughtful Christians who are "trying to believe in a time of the death of God." The "Augustinian-Reformed" picture of a God of transcendence is problematic to modern man. Not only have the idols or the falsely objectivized idea of God died, in Hamilton's view; there is also the "death in us of any power to affirm the traditional images of God."[23] This strangely poignant and pathetic posture draws from Hamilton a starkly limited theological statement: God "seems to have withdrawn from the world and its sufferings, and this leads us to accuse him of either irrelevance or cruelty. But in another sense, he is experienced as a pressure and a wounding from which we would love to be free. For many of us who call ourselves Christians, therefore, believing in the time of the 'death of God' means that he is there when we do not want him, in ways we do not want him, and he is not there when we do want him."[24] The "pressure" we feel is that which calls us to responsible, humble, neighborly existence in a world come of age. Theology essentially is an acknowledgment of Jesus' lordship over the world as a lordship of humiliation (our present existence) and a lordship of victory (our hope). The Christian's religious stance is primarily an extension of his sense for the humiliated and victorious Lord who alone survives the "death of God."

d. *The New Christology.* Paul van Buren's study, *The Secular Meaning of the Gospel,*[25] also acknowledges the "this-worldly" aspect of the gospel. Like Hamilton, van Buren shares the modern temper which assumes the inadequacy of theological language. Whereas Hamilton seems to return to the barest statement of the meaningful ethic of Jesus, van Buren proposes to attack the problem of theological language by bringing the latter to terms with other modes of contemporary thinking, particularly linguistic analysis. "Linguistic analysis exposes the function of language in just those areas on which modern theology seeks to shed light: the world in which the 'average' Christian finds himself."[26] In effect, van Buren reduces Christian faith to historical and ethical dimensions. To critics who would ask for more, he responds: "What more?" Rejecting both the theological right with its emphasis upon the concrete event in Jesus Christ and the theological left with its emphasis upon analogy, van Buren proposes a theology in which the history of Jesus of Nazareth is the central interpretation and in which the relationship between faith and Jesus must lie in Easter.

e. *The New Metaphysics.* John B. Cobb, Jr., while

clearly recognizing the shape of the current situation in theology, rejects the antimetaphysical trend of most of the "death of God" exposition. He points out that many of the alternatives amidst the passing of crisis theology appear to "return to that relativistic sea from which crisis theology seemed briefly to save us."[27] Noting that much contemporary theology, and indeed contemporary self-consciousness, assumes the problematic character of the objective realm, Cobb correctly reminds us that we do not in fact enjoy even subjective certainty. If we did, the recognition of objective certainty would not be such a serious question. Cobb insists that the serious task before theology is therefore the "question of objective warrant" which "can no longer be pushed aside."[28] He turns to Alfred North Whitehead's "new world": "Whitehead's earlier work reflects the death of God at least by its silence. But it gradually became clear as his philosophical speculations broadened that the philosophical reasons for the death of God were repudiated by him. Hence once again the questions of being and becoming emerged in his thought in such a way as to cry for belief in God."[29] Thus Cobb, in distinction from the other thinkers referred to, is seriously in search of a new "Christian natural theology" on Whiteheadian presuppositions. Speaking for himself and a whole generation of younger theologians, Cobb urges serious attention to theological problems: "In our day we must run fast if we would stand still, and faster still if we would catch up. We can only hope that we will be granted both time and courage."[30]

IV

The sense of the "death of God" is a pervasive mood in contemporary thought, and this, inevitably, is the context in which theology exists and works. In the recognition of the seriousness of this spiritual crisis in Western culture lies the hope for Christian thought and experience. To dismiss the problem of the "death of God" as irrelevant or academic would be to fly in the face of the vast secular witness to the withdrawal of the reality of God from contemporary experience. On the other hand, to suggest, as some do, that discussion of this situation obscures the Christian sense of life, is to be equally overzealous in quest of a pattern.

The "death of God" image points to a "style" in contemporary theology and philosophy that is usually antimetaphysical, earnestly moral, and hopefully secular. The varieties of uses of the term are apparent. But the expression reveals an indisputable fact. What was a powerful metaphor in the hands of Nietzsche has become in our time a rallying slogan for the widespread restlessness regarding traditional ways of speaking about the God who is no longer apprehended in meaningful ways. Truly ours is a world in which truth and reality seem to have collapsed into relativity. The "death of God," despite the speculations of Nietzsche and Dostoevsky, has ushered in, not the age of man, but rather the age of anxiety, alienation, irrationalism, and boredom. Here is, in truth, the "death of man" as a self-conscious and responsible individual.

Recognition of this crisis of faith has led theologians to use the striking expression of Nietzsche as an announcement of a situation to which they must address themselves. But a proclamation is at best a provisional or propaedeutic gesture. There are signs that the stimulus of the Nietzschean tradition will create a "new breed" of Christian theologian who will heed Cobb's plea "to reach out for a novelty that disdains all appeal to the authority of the past and dares to think creatively and constructively in the present."[31]

NOTES

1. J. A. T. Robinson, *Honest to God* (The Westminster Press, 1963).

2. Martin Buber, *Eclipse of God* (Harper & Brothers, 1952), p. 20.

3. Cf. Franklin Baumer, *Religion and the Rise of Skepticism* (Harcourt, Brace and World, Inc., 1960).

4. J. Hillis Miller, *The Disappearance of God* (Harvard University Press, 1964), p. 13.

5. Margaret Maison, *The Victorian Vision* (Sheed & Ward, Inc., 1963), p. 209.

6. *Ibid.*, p. 210.

7. Carl Becker, *The Heavenly City of the Eighteenth-Century Philosophers* (Yale University Press, 1932), p. 73.

8. Friedrich Nietzsche, "The Gay Science," in *Existentialism from Dostoyevsky to Sartre*, ed. by Walter Kaufmann (Meridian Books, 1956), p. 105.

9. Fyodor Dostoevsky, *The Possessed* (Dell Publishing Company, 1961), p. 133.

10. Nietzsche, *Thus Spoke Zarathustra* (Henry Regnery Company, 1957), p. 97.

11. Thomas Langan, *The Meaning of Heidegger* (Columbia University Press, 1959), p. 191.

12. Buber, *op. cit.*, p. 14.

13. Cf. William Barrett, *Irrational Man* (Doubleday & Company, Inc., 1958), p. 205.

14. Quoted by James Eadie, "The Absence of God," in *Christianity and Existentialism*, ed. by John Wild (Northwestern University Press, 1963), p. 137.

15. *Ibid.*, p. 121.

16. Martin Heidegger, *Erläuterungen zu Hölderlins Dichtung*, 2nd ed., p. 44, quoted by James M. Robinson, *The Later Heidegger and Theology* (Harper & Row, Publishers, Inc., 1963), p. 14.

17. Cf. Buber, *op. cit.*, p. 23.

18. *Ibid.*, p. 68.

19. Gabriel Vahanian, *The Death of God: The Culture of Our Post-Christian Era* (George Braziller, 1961).

20. Vahanian, "The Future of Christianity in a Post-Christian Era," *The Centennial Review*, Vol. VIII, No. 2 (Spring, 1964), p. 161.

21. Thomas J. J. Altizer, "Theology and the Death of God," *The Centennial Review*, Vol. VIII, No. 2 (Spring, 1964), p. 132.

22. *Ibid.*, p. 145.

23. William Hamilton, *The New Essence of Christianity* (Association Press, 1961), p. 58.

24. *Ibid.*, p. 65.

25. Paul van Buren, *The Secular Meaning of the Gospel* (The Macmillan Company, 1963).

26. *Ibid.*, p. 195.

27. John B. Cobb, Jr., "From Crisis Theology to Post-Modern World," *The Centennial Review*, Vol. VIII, No. 2 (Spring, 1964), p. 178.

28. Cobb, *Living Options in Protestant Theology* (The Westminster Press, 1962), p. 317.

29. Cobb, "From Crisis Theology to Post-Modern World," p. 183

30. Cobb, *Living Options in Protestant Theology*, p. 323.

31. Cobb, "From Crisis Theology to Post-Modern World," p. 181.

Daniel Callahan

RADICAL THEOLOGY
OR RADICAL TITILLATION?

I THINK one can take it for granted
that any radically new theological
movement is going to seem offensive. This is doubly true
of what William Hamilton has called the "death of God"
theologies. Not only do they mark a sharp break with
most traditional and contemporary theology, but they
would also enthrone as their starting point a denial of
that belief which has hitherto given theology its *raison
d'être:* that God lives. The English philosopher Ninian
Smart has expressed a suitably wry scorn: "A colleague
of mine recently said to me: 'My wife is an atheist, but
she wants to be an Anglican as well. Is there anything
she can read?' 'My dear fellow,' I replied, 'we've got
plenty of books showing how the trick can be done.'"

The word "trick" sounds just right here. What else can
be said of a "theology" (for they continue to use the
word) which: (1) appears to take literally the linguistically nonsensical phrase "God is dead," (2) shares with
the atheist an unwillingness to take seriously anything
outside of man and nature, and then (3) has the ef-
frontery to assert that it may be possible to give this
outlook a Biblical basis? One is likely to feel at this point

Previously unpublished.

much like Kai Nielsen felt after trying to make some sense of Paul Tillich: "Tillich doesn't put new wine into old bottles, he puts in grape soda and then labels it *Chateau Latour*."

One way or the other, the "death of God" theologies invite a hostile response; only after one has vented one's spleen can calmness return and a second, more positive, look be taken. A good way to begin the assault would be to accent with full solemnity the claim of Hamilton and Altizer that we are secular men, men for whom the Christian God no longer lives. Well, if I am a secular man, then the "death of God" makes no more sense than the earlier talk about the "living God." In "The Shape of a Radical Theology" (*The Christian Century,* Oct. 6, 1965), Hamilton wrote that the value of the expression "God is dead" is that it suggests a "real loss, something irretrievable"; that is the value of using the metaphor of death. By contrast, other phrases, such as the "absence of God" (Heidegger), the "eclipse of God" (Buber), or the "hidden God" of the tradition, lack sufficient decisiveness. They "still live quite comfortably within the classical tradition of the dialectic between the presence and absence of God."

What in the world could *any* of this mean to secular man? Since he has a notoriously literal mind, secular man would at once be likely to ask how the traditional God, who was by definition omnipotent, eternal, and uncreated, could in any sense be said to have "died." Only those capable of death can die, but the very meaning of the word "God" in traditional terms entailed the impossibility of death. At least, "God died" or "God is dead" is a logical contradiction. Of course the whole point of secular man's existence is that he refuses at the outset to get involved in any kind of talk about God. He could only chuckle to hear theologians solemnly discuss the death of a God who never made any sense to him in the first place. How can what never was and never could be die? Ridiculous, the whole business.

But let us imagine that secular man somehow managed a supreme act of permissiveness toward the odd logic of the "death of God" theologians. He would still have many problems. Hamilton, for instance, denies that his position can be equated with classical atheism. In "The Death of God Theologies Today," Hamilton writes that there "is an element of expectation, even hope, that removes my position from classical atheisms and that even removes it from a large amount of anguish and gloom." He then goes on to talk about "waiting for God."

"Come now," secular man would have to say at this point, "how can you talk about waiting for a God who has been declared dead?" If he is dead, then he wasn't God in the first place. But if he can come back from the dead—if it makes any sense at all to talk about "waiting" for him—then he must not really be dead at all (or "dead" only in some odd sense of the word). If God can "die" and then bring himself back to life, we are right back where we started: with an omnipotent, eternal God. Hamilton's "hope" and his "waiting" make sense, then, only on the presupposition that the supposed "death of God" is not quite the radical and final event he proclaims it to be. (And was it a slip of the pen or a hedging of his bet which led Hamilton at the end of his essay on "The Death of God Theologies Today" to speak of "waiting for the absent God"? "Absent"? The whole point of the essay, one was led to believe, was that God was gone and gone for good.) Nor could secular man be anything but amused by Hamilton's vague affection for the figure of Jesus. The traditional Jesus made an odd kind of sense, that Jesus who was the Word made flesh, who died for man's sins, who was resurrected, and who dwells eternally in glory with the Father. But a solely ethical Jesus? Why him and not some other ethical model? Hamilton never really tells us, except that somehow commitment to this Jesus is supposed to enable one to affirm the world. Perhaps for some anachronistic Christian world deniers all of this is terribly radical. For secular man it is nothing but sugar on his sweet pudding.

Altizer would fare no better at the hands of secular man. In his article in *The Christian Century*, "Creative Negation in Theology" (July 7, 1965), Altizer said that "the Word of faith is now silent. Linger as we may with its vanishing echo, we are nevertheless confronted with the necessity of either desperately clinging to a past moment of the Word or of opening ourselves to a radically new form of faith." Just what kind of "necessity" is involved here? Surely it is not necessary for secular man to open himself to "a radically new form of faith"; there are many other options available to him, including the option of no faith at all. As for the Christian, why should he not just become an ex-Christian? If his earlier faith has now failed, is there any guarantee whatsoever that this new one will fare any better? Why not just affirm the world—what else is there?—rid oneself of excess theological baggage (i.e., all of it), and live the best kind of life one can? Why get involved once again in any kind of "faith"? In any case, Altizer's love of paradox, his mystical affirmations and negations are extraordinarily difficult for secular man to understand. "If ours is truly a history in which God is no longer present, then we are called upon not simply to accept the death of God with Stoic fortitude but rather to will the death of God with the passion of faith." What? If God is dead, he is dead. How in the world can one "will" the death of one who is in fact dead?

Paul van Buren poses somewhat different problems. The first is whether it is proper to speak of him as a "death of God" theologian at all. This may well be doubted, for despite Hamilton's inclusion of his name and work in his piece "The Death of God Theologies Today," it is clear his thought patterns are very different from those of Hamilton and Altizer. For one thing, he saw at the outset that the phrase "God is dead" is linguistically meaningless: there is no conceivable way of verifying the supposed demise of God and thus no way to give the phrase meaningful content. For another, van Buren is too hardheaded and too consistent to be caught "waiting" for a dead God or to take flight with Altizer toward some sublime *coincidentia oppositorum* wherein the profane will be resurrected "in a transfigured and finally sacred form."

But if van Buren is not, strictly speaking, on the staff of President Hamilton's New School, there is still a sense in which he could be called an adjunct professor. For if one is going to speak, with Altizer, of willing the death of God, then van Buren is well able to supply some homicidal instruments for those who want to proceed in a systematic fashion. Unlike Hamilton, van Buren is very clear about his secular starting point and his methodology. The task he sets himself in *The Secular Meaning of the Gospel* is to interpret the gospel in an empirical way. That is the way men think today, and it is just as legitimate to attempt a translation of the gospel into empirical terms as it was for earlier Christians to attempt a translation into Platonic or Aristotelian or Kantian or Hegelian terms. "How," he asks, "can a Christian who is himself a secular man understand the Gospel in a secular way?" The question is a shrewd one and van Buren's answer is direct: "We must begin where we can, with the realm of the world, open in principle to human investigation, and that means, Christologically speaking, with the true humanity of Jesus of Nazareth." Even more concretely, the tool of linguistic analysis must be brought to bear; it provides a superb instrument for implementing a decision to remain consistently empirical and secular.

Van Buren's questions, though, are more interesting
than his answers. As one might foresee at the outset, the
resultant "secular meaning of the gospel" is dull and un-
interesting. This is the usual fate of reductionist interpretations of almost any complex phenomena. Interces-
sory prayer, for instance, comes down to a reflecting on
problems from a Christian perspective and then taking
appropriate action. One can only say in response, yawning all the while, "That's very interesting." A more glaring
weakness, however, and the most revealing, is van Buren's
dependence upon two of the least impressive of the
English analysts, at least so far as their analysis of religious language and concepts are concerned, R. M. Hare
and R. B. Braithwaite. From Hare, he takes the notion of
"bliks," a word meant to signify a person's fundamental
attitudes, his basic presuppositions, about the world. Religious assertions are not to be understood as assertions
capable of verification or falsification, but as expressive
only of ultimate attitudes and orientations. Hence for
Hare it is inappropriate to ask whether religious assertions are true or false. Braithwaite's position, fully expressed in *An Empiricist's View of Religious Belief*, is
that religious assertions are nothing more than disguised
moral assertions: they do not state facts, or tell us anything about the world, but are instead used to guide
our conduct.

There is something to be said for each of these positions, but they both suffer the fatal deficiency of trying
to find a single, central use of religious concepts and
language. They thus represent the more primitive phase
of twentieth-century analysis, only a shade more sophisticated than the early A. J. Ayer. If the later work of the
analysts has clarified anything, it is that there are many
different uses of religious concepts and language and that
only a contextual analysis can show precisely how they
are being used in any given case. Hare, Braithwaite, and

van Buren see clearly that the positivists were naïve in attempting to judge religious language by the standards of the empirical sciences, but none of them seems to see that it is equally naïve to search for archetypal uses of religious utterances.

It may seem something of a digression to mention the way in which van Buren relies upon the philosophers who attract him. Yet I think not. The test of any recourse to secular insights is how they work in practice, in their application to the theological matter at hand. A fatal error of the nervous theologian is to rule out a priori certain approaches—that is why the very idea of a "secular interpretation of the gospel" has been dismissed in so many quarters as preposterous. The history of theology, however, is a history of mixed marriages; the families groaned but the marriages often turned out beautifully. Van Buren's failure does not lie in trying to work from a secular perspective, but in failing to show that it will work successfully. He is quite right in reminding us that "Christians were once called atheists by a misunderstanding, but religious, culture." Yet he does not achieve his own stated aim: "an interpretation which may claim for a secular Christianity the full tradition of the faith." If nothing else, that tradition has always held that there is a reality which transcends that which is open to empirical investigation and understanding. One may say the tradition was wrongheaded on the point, but it was still part of the tradition.

William Hamilton has complained with much effectiveness about those philosophers (e.g., Alasdair MacIntyre) who smugly insist that the radical theologians are nothing but covert atheists. His point is well taken, but it would be even more persuasive if he showed greater sensitivity to the possibility that the radical theologians are engaged in a vast attempt to save what cannot be saved. A reading into the Christian tradition of elements which are not there, or a systematic overlooking of elements which are, could well be taken as behavioral symptoms of this rationalization. Though Altizer's work is heavily laden with religious fantasy he is at least candid enough to admit, in *The Sacred and the Profane,* that the "dialectical understanding of the Incarnation" which he espouses "must go beyond the New Testament" and that a "theology which remains bound to the language and imagery of the New Testament must refuse the very thesis that the Incarnation is a forward movement of process." More admissions of this kind by the radical theologians would do much to exonerate them from the charge of being self-deceivers who have mishaped historical Christianity into their own theological image.

As I mentioned at the outset, there is much about the "death of God" theologians worth an angry outburst. They can be criticized on secular grounds for proclaiming secularity but then failing to live up to its radical demands—its merciless logic, its dislike of sweeping visions, its devastating use of Ockham's razor, its refusal to entertain sheerly voluntaristic hopes. They can be criticized on Christian grounds for departing from Scripture while only rarely conceding they do so; for taking contemporary secularity as a norm by which to measure theology rather than the other way around; for being captives of the intellectual power structures of secular man; for failing to show a sufficient awareness of the subtleties of historical theology. To say this much is, for me at least, to exhaust most of my hostility.

There is also a good word to be said. On the purely literal level, it is exceedingly difficult to be persuaded that the "death of God" theologians (with the possible exception of van Buren) even make sense. There seems, then, little advantage in replacing the contradictions and obscurantism of traditional Christianity with a new set of contradictions and obscurantism. The only question which remains is this: Is it possible to demythologize their work and thus discover what they are trying to say? What lies behind their culturally conditioned myths, their time-bound language, their emotive proclamations of God's death? What is their central insight, and what question does this insight answer?

An immediate perplexity is that each of the three theologians discussed here actually works from very different premises. Despite their apparent agreement that "God is dead," Hamilton and Altizer live in different intellectual worlds. And van Buren lives in still another. That much said by way of caution, at least a few generalizations may be ventured. For all three the word "God" corresponds to nothing in their experience; it literally signifies a blank, but a blank which nonetheless has an effective content. When Hamilton and Altizer say that "God is dead" they are only saying as much; or at least, that is what they are trying to say once one sees through their unsuccessful attempt to state in the objective, empirical mode a report about their subjective experience. For this reason, Hamilton is most intelligible when he says, "We are talking . . . about the experience of the absence of God." By dramatizing this "experience," by trying to give it a shape and direction, they have made an important contribution. No one can tell how pervasive is this experience among contemporary Christians, but it is surely common to many; it is good that a few theologians have brought this fact out into the open.

Working from this experience of absence, they ask the question whether it is possible for one to be a Christian without an awareness of God or a sense of the transcendent. Can Christianity be uprooted from its historical and metaphysical soil while still remaining in some legitimate sense "Christianity"? This question has been asked before, but almost always in the context of a steady faith in God, a present or recollected experience of God, or some rational indications of God's existence and nature. But what does one do if this faith and experience are dead and the word "God" itself has become just a noise pointing to nothing at all? More precisely, what does one do if all of these things are so—and yet the Jesus of Scripture remains a powerful, mysterious, and unique person, who cannot be contained within the categories of that secularity and worldliness which seem so triumphant and persuasive? That is the question, the real question, which I think the "death of God" theologians are asking. Thus put, it is a question which gives their quixotic verbal behavior a consistency which, on the face of it, appears totally lacking. They want to deny God while holding on to Jesus; but the Jesus they seek is not a Jesus cut down to human size—the consummate secular man—but a Jesus who will once again lead man out of the wilderness of the dead past and the specious present into the eschatological future. This impulse toward a fresh faith is almost inchoate in Hamilton; yet it is there. It is far more articulated in Altizer. By the "death of God" he means that movement of God from radical transcendence to radical immanence. The transcendent God of the tradition died to give life to the immanent God in Jesus: the "Incarnate Word . . . empties itself of Spirit so as to appear and exist as flesh." Once flesh, this Word will not return to the primordial beginning; it is a Word in process, moving toward an "eschatological *coincidentia oppositorum*," that is, "a coming together or dialectical union of an original sacred and the radical profane." Altizer would have us do that which is, in the end, the hardest thing of all for secular man: "sense the possibility of a Yes which can become a No, and of a No which can become a Yes." Herein, according to Altizer, lies the "scandal" of faith.

The word "scandal" is important. A central thrust of

the tradition, the "scandal" of Christianity—or better, of Jesus Christ—must be preserved. Hamilton comes closest to emptying it of all content. His Jesus shocks in only the most pedestrian sort of way, the way a member of SNCC might initially shock a white suburbanite. One can admire, but hardly place one's faith in this Jesus. Altizer's Jesus, by contrast, is a person to reckon with, one who transcends and transforms history (and not just corrupt power structures). While it is still not evident just where van Buren's work will take him, his Jesus of *The Secular Meaning of the Gospel* suffers from some of the same insipidity which is shot through Hamilton's writing. There is no "scandal" there, just mild surprise.

Does the "death of God" movement (and is it even that?) have a future? I doubt it, but if it succeeds at least in calling attention to the contemporary Christian's "experience of the absence of God," it will have served a valuable purpose. Beyond that, if it can locate more effectively wherein the permanent scandal of Christianity lies—wherein, to be precise, the figure of Jesus Christ can still be a scandal to secular man and those who follow secular man—then it will well justify the hoopla it instigated. For the fate of the prophet today is likely to be fame and fortune, headlines in the press, and a flattering dismemberment by dozens of colloquiums. The ability of Hamilton and Altizer to survive these rigors will be a measure of their theological vitality, and the staying power of what they have to say. If Altizer can imitate the tough-mindedness of van Buren; if van Buren can gain some of Altizer's sensitivity to the sacred; if Hamilton can develop a philosophical or theological system (as did Altizer and van Buren) to support his exhortations— in that event, then, we may have the makings of a genuine revolution. At the moment, we still only have something new to talk about.

Arthur Hertzberg

JEWS
AND THE DEATH OF GOD

WILLIAM HAMILTON's recent essay, "Radicalism and the Death of God" (Dec. 13, 1965), is beginning to convince me that the "death of God" theologians do represent at least the beginnings of a serious new movement within Christianity. Like the young Luther, Hamilton displays one of the certain signs of a revolution in Christian theology: he turns to the Jews to reopen discussions in a new way, saying that "some connection may be discernible between the death of God theology and the Jew today."

All is not yet clear in Hamilton's own mind, but he has a hunch that a radical Christianity, one that has abandoned the theological formulas of the past, can much more easily talk with Judaism. It is no long step for a Christian (and Hamilton is one, by history, culture, and feeling, if no longer by classic theology) to arrive at the next stage, the one to which the absolutist Luther came immediately and in a very direct line. At the end of his life Luther was thundering at the obdurate Jews for refusing to accept his purified Christianity.

Such an attitude is not completely unthinkable even

From *Christianity and Crisis*, February 7, 1966. Reprinted by permission.

among Christians who have abandoned orthodox theological beliefs. For at least a century some of the forerunners of the new "death of God" school managed to be quite testy about the persistence of the Jews. Renan was annoyed with them for having failed to accept the man Jesus and thus, in his view, for having condemned themselves to becoming a backwater in the history of human culture.

This attitude is probably the root of Toynbee's famous view that Judaism is a "fossil." He himself is a post-Christian syncretist, but the Jews who rejected Christianity are, for him, a people who failed to keep pace with the advance of humanity. Boris Pasternak, of Jewish origin and not in any theological sense a believing Christian, argued the same point several times in *Dr. Zhivago:* the Jews have no present reason for standing aside from the morality, traditions, and art of Christian culture, even though Pasternak took none of its symbols with any literalness.

On the American scene some of the most advanced theological liberals and "social gospelers" of the last two generations (e.g., Norman Thomas) have been passionately anti-Zionist on the grounds that any affirmation of separate Jewish identity was reactionary. Christians of this stripe tended to think that the world needed the resolution of the ancient tensions between the Christian and the Jewish traditions in a new age of untheological moral idealism, of which Jesus the man was the chief prophet. Jews are perhaps candidates for atheism, but not for Christian atheism.

In two senses Jewish experience may be relevant to those who are trying to formulate the "death of God" outlook. For at least a century Jews have been dealing with the problem of defining themselves as Jews in the midst of the evaporation of the classic faith. Precisely because Judaism was the religion of an embattled minority, disbelieving Jews could not leave their community as easily as disbelieving Christians could.

Advanced Jewish intellectuals, from Moses Hess to David Ben-Gurion, have generally affirmed not the theology of Judaism but the history and evolving experience of the Jewish people as the ultimate value they venerate. This vision has been one of a world made up of all its historic communities, united by common moral purpose, indifferent to theology, and separated by their roots in their various histories.

Mr. Hamilton and his colleagues might possibly be responding to the twin crises of Christianity—the evaporating faith of its own intellectuals and the end of its missionary hopes in any foreseeable future—by moving comparably. Their theology may thus amount to an affirmation of a cultural Christianity willing to live as one among many cultures, nourished by some pride in the history of Christianity and Christendom, while freeing itself from the doctrines and the memories it does not find inspiring.

That is essentially the path to a Christian equivalent of Jewish cultural Zionism, and I recommend that these theologians read such people as Ahad-Ha-Am, much of whose work has been translated into English by Sir Leon Simon. In his essay on Moses, this late nineteenth-century Russian Jewish thinker asserts that the historicity of Moses is irrelevant because his image has been central to the making of unique Jewish history. I can imagine Hamilton saying the same about Jesus—but it has, of course, already been said in Christian Europe a century ago.

I am worried by Hamilton's assertion that "the believing Jew is the man with God and without the Messiah: the death of God Protestant is the man without God but not without something like the Messiah." On purely theological grounds the statement about Judaism is not true. The whole of Judaism is, religiously, the history of waiting for the Messiah who has not yet come. This is no abstraction. Almost every contemporary Jew had a grandfather who slept every night of his life fully dressed, to be able to follow the Messiah if he came during the night. It was this hope for the future that sustained Jews through their many dark presents.

I am even more worried by Mr. Hamilton's other assertion, which implies that he has "something like the Messiah" to offer Jews. Jews have lived through quite a number of Messianic upsurges within Christianity and Islam. After a while each of these deistic movements calmed down sufficiently to agree that Jews should be allowed to work out their own religious salvation. It was discovered that the absolute God who had commanded the Messianists was opposed to the use of religious coercion.

I hope that the absent God of the newest theological currents will command his followers against the pride of the new and against cultural imperialism. What I hope they are really talking about as Christians is an acceptance of the world in which we live, in which we can survive together only in humility.

J. A. Sanders

BIBLICAL FAITH
AND
THE DEATH OF GOD MOVEMENT

THE "DEATH OF GOD" movement claims to be indigenous to our American shores. Certainly it is one of the most exhilarating modes of theological thinking to strike these shores in modern times. Never has there been, I think, in Christian theological circles, headier thinking, frothier enthusiasm, or more sheer giddiness. The most vigorous radical of them all, Thomas J. J. Altizer of Emory, at times, in his writing, seems to be executing a primitive choreographic joy, and, like Snoopy in "Peanuts," twirls around and around singing his Easter message, "God is dead, God is dead."[1] Thinkers like Altizer claim that they are the true Christians and that all who react against his kenotic Christology are the orthodox bad guys who are not Christian at all. Others among them, like Paul van Buren of Temple, and William Hamilton of Colgate Rochester, while no less clear in proclaiming the "death of God," show considerably more hesitation and wonderment at what is happening to them. John B. Cobb, Jr., and Harvey Cox, as well as other so-called Christian relativists and secularists, are not to be confused with the genuine "death

From "The Vitality of the Old Testament," *Union Seminary Quarterly Review*, January, 1966. Used by permission.

of God" group.[2] The secularists claim that the theological vocabulary of orthodoxy is dead and must be completely altered, whereas the radicals claim that God is dead and Christianity must be completely altered. Altizer thinks that his kenotic Christology has never heretofore been expressed: "Until this day Christian theology has refused a consistently kenotic Christology. Yet an open confession of the death of God can be our path to the Christ who is fully Christ, the kenotic Christ who has finally emptied himself of Spirit in wholly becoming flesh."[3] For William Hamilton, God is man's idea of a problem-solver who has completely failed: he simply hasn't solved any problems and is therefore dead.[4] But Jesus is not dead, for Hamilton. On the contrary, Jesus is playing hide-and-seek out in the world somewhere and the game is to go out into the world and tear off his mask. "Jesus is in the world as masked, and the work of the Christian is to strip off the masks of the world to find him, and finding him, to stay with him and to do his work.... Life is a masked ball, a Halloween party, and the Christian life, ethics, love, is that disruptive task of tearing off the masks of the guests to discover the true princess."[5] Altizer's Christ who is pure flesh, and Hamilton's Jesus who is the true Princess, make the world which they cherish as truth, sound like a Hefner Bunny Club to which Christians can now belong with no feelings of guilt or shirking of Calvinist duty.

Fortunately, the "death of God" movement has an interpreter, sometimes called its scribe, who is not himself one of their number, Langdon Gilkey of Chicago. While the actual adherents are out there in their world "becoming Jesus," as Hamilton would say, Gilkey makes his acute observations from the sidelines.[6] It is Gilkey who has shown most clearly how the "death of God" movement has grown out of Barthian neo-orthodoxy, a point which Hamilton agrees to and accepts.[7] (Hamilton, my former colleague of eleven years, was until five years ago a thoroughgoing Barthian, a fact which even his *The New Essence of Christianity* of 1961 did not dispel.) But Gilkey has also shown their indebtedness to Tillich and Bultmann as well.[8]

The radicals have seemingly accepted the very points of thinking in Barth, Tillich, and Bultmann which Biblical scholars and careful Biblical theologians have been reluctant to accept from those giants of the past generation. The Christocentrism of Barth's essentially dualistic cosmology, the nontheist ontology of Tillich, and the existentialist spiritualizing of Biblical images in Bultmann are precisely those contributions of the past generation most puzzling and unacceptable to Biblical students (that is, of course, students of the whole Bible).

The balancing positive elements in the thinking of these three greats, Gilkey goes on, "do not seem consciously to influence the new [theologians]." Those positive elements are precisely the lessons grasped and accepted by Biblical theologians, namely, "the emphasis on God, revelation and the word in Barth; on an ontological analysis of existential 'depth,' on revelation and on Being itself in Tillich; and on existential inwardness and self-understanding 'at the boundary' and 'before God' in Bultmann."[9] But it appears that it has been their negative, the netherside, contributions which have come to the fore in the radicals: Barth's Christocentric particularity as over against God's universal sovereignty and reign; and Tillich's and Bultmann's finding God only out at the frontier or edge of existence and not in ordinary living. Unwittingly each man seemed to deny God's immediate reign and sovereignty in the common stuff of life, the world into which the radicals now summon us to follow in exuberance.

Accepting this separation of holy and secular,[10] the radicals claim that truth is to be found not in the sacred special places of Word, Christ, and Church but in the ordinary places of the profane world where Jesus actually is and has been all along. All the nonverifiable and non-propositional truth of theology, eschatology, and myth-ology is completely rejected in favor of the verifiable, provable world.

I should like to record both my positive reactions to and my serious criticisms of the new theology. First and foremost, I admire and support their intellectual honesty. This is perhaps their strongest asset. They are saying out loud, in many ways, the honest reservations we are all harboring in the haven of faith. They are willing to express on their feet what we have all been pondering in our swivel chairs. Armed with such honesty they might just happen to be, for today, God's special people, his elite guard of madmen, his prophets of our day with the tongues of sword, his cherished iconoclasts of established thinking. In the face of such a force of intellectual honesty what they say cannot be ignored, no matter how outlandish it may seem. Those twins of falsehood which forever crouch at the door of faith, credulity and hypoc-risy, cannot long remain lodged among us when prophets are on the loose. Is it not at the heart of the Old Testa-ment to hear the prophets say, your view of God is not God — he isn't here, he's there; he's way ahead of you; nothing you think about him touches him; your thoughts are not his thoughts? For God is mobile, not static; he is itinerant, not stable; he is forever active, not immutable. (He told Moses of the Children of Israel, "Go tell them I'll be there." And the women at the tomb were informed, "He is not here.") God is forever outside our beliefs about him. The orthodox belief we may pretend to have is itself under the judgment of God. One can only thank God for the intellectual honesty of the "death of God" theologians.

Secondly, I appreciate their affirmation of the world, the whole world I hope—and not just Hamilton's "pro-bourgeois, urban and political" worldliness, not only

Cox's "technopolis," but the whole world in all its aspects, the whole of creation and all of human experience. Here especially is the Old Testament truth of the wholeness of life being restated by the radicals. The so-called ethical dualism of the Hellenistic and New Testament writings needs periodically to come under the judgment of Old Testament thinking. Harvey Cox has, at least partially, understood that the faith of Israel was a secularization of ancient Near Eastern thinking, a desacralization of all creation myths, a proclamation that God and his world are all there is.[11] The world is good because it is whole.

Thirdly, I acclaim the iconoclasm of the new theology. If their *Wait Without Idols*[12] can truly be a waiting on the Lord, without idolatry, then let us pray that he will indeed renew their strength. By iconoclasm I mean not so much the destruction of our conventional understanding of idols, apostasy, and sin, though that is ever-present; I mean rather the comfortable ingroup thinking into which we have cozied our minds so that we have somehow managed to convince ourselves that salvation comes by jargon and slogan. If the young Turks shall but cause us to reexamine our established vocabulary and the settled theology of the establishment, they shall have effected a blessing upon us all. But even more important a boon might issue from an honest reappraisal of the relationship and interaction between the God of the Bible and the God of Christian metaphysics. For all our much-touted "Return to the Bible" in the past forty years have we honestly subjected the God of Western speculation to the judgment of the Biblical God? There are a number of us stubborn students of the Bible who think not. If with Barth what we have managed to do is somehow to separate God from his world; and if with Tillich we have managed somehow to discount Biblical personal theism; and if with Bultmann we have managed somehow to separate God from the Biblical modes of speaking about him and of praising him—all this, mind you, with the purpose of replacing Biblical thinking with modern understandable and acceptable thinking—then is not the resultant "God" of recent theology already very nearly remade in our image? Could we not have foreseen that a Christian theology which centered itself in an ontologically and existentially acceptable Christ would find its goal in losing its God? Has not Christian theology itself in its excessive Christocentrism perhaps indeed veiled God? Can we really blame Altizer for coming up with his so-called kenotic Christology? "God so loved the world that he died for it." The great hope I see in the new Jesusology is that when, in Hamilton's masked ball, we have found him, we may see something in him, not, pray God, of our kenotic and empty selves, but of the inexhaustible grace of God which, like the Syrian widow's cruse of oil, is always full, and that we finally may see in him the Biblical Jesus who claimed nothing for himself. Then may we develop a truly theocentric Christology and set aside all vain attempts at a Christocentric theology.

But while I am very excited by the possibilities for truth, in the sense of the Greek word for truth, *alētheia*, which etymologically means unveiling or unmasking, as in Hamilton's Halloween party, I must take issue with three of their most basic tenets.

First, while I admire their honesty[13] and feel that it will be an offense to our false faces and masks, I greatly fear that they have made of their honesty a god. The Biblical God is not subject to the judgments of man's honesty; man's honesty is the subject of God's judgments. Have we not yet learned that the honesty we cherish today will tomorrow be seen as dishonesty? The next generation will look upon our soul-searching honesty of today with the same disdain by which we look back upon our Barthian or even our liberal-Victorian honesty. Bertrand Russell, of all people, made my point in his essay

"On Being Modern-minded": "Our age," said Russell, "is the most parochial since Homer. . . . New catchwords hide from us the thoughts and feelings of our ancestors, even when they differed little from our own. We imagine ourselves at the apex of intelligence. . . . There must be something which is felt to be of more importance than the admiration of the contemporary crowd."[14] The "death of God" movement bears the earmarks of being perhaps the most parochial school of thought in all modern theological searching. By their own insistence they are peculiarly an American movement. They claim to want to free American theology from the domination of European attitudes. I find here a strange sort of theological isolationism. But by parochial I mean not only their desire to incubate their ideas in their own heat, I mean also their disdain of history. John B. Cobb pleads for a new breed of Christian theologian who will "reach out for a novelty that disdains all appeal to the authority of the past and dares to think creatively and constructively in the present."[15] I hope that they shall do so, for experimentation can only help in giving birth to new thoughts. But certainly man's honesty cannot lead to a denial of God. Man's honesty can lead only to a recognition of the limitations of man's honesty. Man's honesty, to be honest, is judged by God. I have doubts aplenty; but I, for one, doubt man's omniscience considerably more than I doubt God's.

My second stricture on the new theology is directed at their kenotic Christology, or Jesusology. God, like a good friend, has laid down his life for us. One must remember that these Christian radicals are not atheists, nor are they agnostic. They have more beliefs than most of us; what they believe is not that there is no god but that God has died for us. They might be called ultra-orthodox literalists. They believe in the incarnation without a stopper. In the foreword to his novel *A Death in the Family,*

James Agee described a summer evening in his boyhood neighborhood when all the fathers on the block, in their suspenders, quietly watered their lawns with the garden hoses, which when turned off were "left empty, like God, by the sparrow's fall." The radicals do not bother with the ontological question of the existence of God.[16] God lived, right enough, but now he is dead. Not like El and the other gods of ancient Near East pantheons, because of old age or battles among the gods, the way Marduk slew Tiamat or Yahweh slew Rahab. But rather, God gave himself, emptied himself, killed himself for man's sake, so that man might mature and come of age. God weaned us. Since man has now come of age, say the radicals, it is finally time to shout the Easter message, "God is dead." And that leaves us with man alone. They accept a basic dualism or radical distinction between the sacred and the profane, between God and the world, in order to be rid of the sacred and to proclaim the death of God. Man and the world are left without God or the gods: man and the world are completely secularized. God as a problem solver is finished, they say. But the providence of God in Biblical terms is not God in the guise of man's trouble-shooter. The providence of God in Biblical terms cuts across man's self-understood wants and needs: his wonders are alien; his gifts are strange (Isa. 28:21). Could we not have foreseen radical theology by our overemphasis on the Lutheran rediscovery of God in Bethlehem's cradle? Have we failed sufficiently to emphasize the *Deus Absconditus* and the judgments of God? God cannot die if he never existed; for according to classical Christian theology God does not exist, he gives existence.

My third stricture is directed against the false dichotomy of sacred and profane whereby the Biblical transcendence of God is in effect ridiculed and man displaces a useless, impotent god, a straw god, bearing no relation to the sovereign God of the Bible. There is a sense in which the central proclamation of the "death of God" movement fits a classic Biblical definition of sin. In the Bible it is God alone who lives; it is man who dies.[17] "He lives" is the central message of Habakkuk in the sixth-century B.C. exile, and it is the central message of the evangelists in the first-century A.D. gospel.[18] No matter what valiant efforts may be exerted to avoid setting man up as his own god, or better, as three billion gods, I fear that that is precisely what the "death of God" groups are likely to do. Paul Tillich has recently said, "The temptation not to accept finitude, but rather to lift one's self to the level of the Unconditioned, the Divine, runs through all history."[19] Only he who fancies man to be god can call his God dead, that is, has convinced himself that there is no truth which transcends man. Only he who thinks that our current honesty is the final honesty can truly believe that God is dead. Does "man come of age" not mean man fancying himself to be God? But he who knows that tomorrow's honesty will stand in judgment over today's honesty, and that the work of Truth or unveiling and un-masking is never done, can truly believe that God is God.

NOTES

1. See, for instance, Altizer's "Creative Negation in Theology," *The Christian Century*, July 7, 1965, pp. 864–867.

2. See *ibid.*, p. 865, where Altizer calls Cobb "one of the new theologians." Cobb's Whiteheadian "absolute relativism" is joined, seemingly, to the Barthian dichotomy of sacred and profane which is so fragilely basic to the whole "death of God" movement; cf. Cobb, "From Crisis Theology to Post-Modern World," *The Centennial Review*, VIII (Michigan State University, 1964), pp. 174–188, esp. pp. 174–179. However, one cannot include Cobb in the "death of God" group but rather, perhaps, among those modulating existentialists for whom, also, "experience is concreteness."

3. Altizer, *loc. cit.*, p. 866.

4. Hamilton, "The Death of God Theology," *Christian Scholar*, XLVIII (1965), pp. 27–48; cf. p. 40.

5. *Ibid.*, pp. 46–47.

6. Langdon B. Gilkey, "Is God Dead?" and "God Is Not Dead," *The Voice* (Bulletin of Crozer Theological Seminary), LVII (1965), pp. 4–11.

7. Hamilton, *op. cit.*, p. 30.

8. Gilkey, *op cit.*, p. 4.

9. *Ibid.*

10. The dichotomy of the sacred and the profane is basic to all the radicals but especially important to Altizer. The most succinct, and perhaps the most helpful, statement of Altizer's position is in his "Theology and the Death of God," *The Centennial Review*, VIII (1964), pp. 129–146.

11. Harvey Cox, *The Secular City* (The Macmillan Company, 1964), pp. 18 ff. Whatever one may think of Cox's book, one should not overlook Cox's recent article, "The New Christian Soldiers," *The Nation*, CCI (1965), pp. 216–220.

12. The title of a book by Gabriel Vahanian, *Wait Without Idols* (George Braziller, 1964). "Waiting on God" is an important aspect of the new theology, especially for Altizer and Hamilton.

13. Or is it autobiographic honesty as Mr. Clifford Green, a graduate student at Union, has privately suggested? Is it perhaps honest navel-staring with the vague conviction that others must be "seeing" the same? Hamilton seems to be saying as much in his article, "The Shape of a Radical Theology," *The Christian Century*, Oct. 6, 1965, pp. 1219–1222.

One cannot (God help him) but wonder whether this movement is not an "honest" product of the frenzy for relevance, and the concomitant lack of emphasis on the classical disciplines, which has gripped theological education in America in the past forty years. Much of the future of Christian theological education may depend precisely on how we react to this extreme challenge of the "all-out present" (cf. Hamilton, "Thursday's Child," *Theology Today*, XX [1964], pp. 487–495): let us hope that the reaction will not itself be frenzied but rather a sober appraisal of the requirements of the next generations as well as of the present.

14. Russell, *Unpopular Essays* (1950), pp. 88–94.

15. Cobb, "From Crisis Theology to Post-Modern World" (see above, note 9), p. 181. Cobb continues, "To refuse the authority of the past need not mean to ignore its truth and reality . . . [the Christian theologian is] avidly open to all truth—yet still believing."

16. See Altizer in *The Centennial Review* article (note 10), pp. 136 ff.

17. Sanders, "God Is God," *Foundations,* VI (1963), pp. 343–361.

18. Sanders, "Thy God Reigneth," *motive,* XVI (February, 1956), pp. 28–31.

19. Paul Tillich, "Frontiers," *Journal of Bible and Religion,* XXXIII (1965), pp. 17–23; see p. 22.

Paul L. Holmer

CONTRA
THE
NEW THEOLOGIES

T O BE INVOLVED vocationally with the
Christian churches is no slight mat-
ter these days; both the theology and the institution of
the church are under constant attack, very often from a
kind of elite group within the family of churches. This
supergroup often has the advantages of feeding on what
looks like the very latest research and modern trends
while simultaneously combining the Christian's awareness of shortcomings before God with a host of obvious
diatribes against ministers, institutions, and policies.
Backed by the prestige of modern learning, a breezy
Protestant theology is developing—strongly antichurch,
opposed to personal piety, occasionally Biblical, very
much this-worldly, almost impervious to criticism. To
oppose this very modern Protestant theology is to risk
being labeled an obscurantist, a fundamentalist, even a
pietist.

I. BEYOND BONHOEFFER?

For this new theology—in large part implicit—is often
more an ethos than a code, more a style than a creed. It is

From *The Christian Century*, March 17, 1965. Copyright 1965
Christian Century Foundation. Reprinted by permission.

found in all denominations and at varying levels, in the "advanced" theological set and also among those who speak to students and informed laymen. Furthermore, it appears to be in advance of the age—the cutting edge of the theological thrust, as it were. Thus, to criticize it makes one seem guilty of obstructing progress. Of course, one must beware of letting age and desire for security motivate one against acceptance of the new. With the world full of cranks whose conservatism comes not from insight but from sheer prejudice, it might seem that strictures against this lively theological and institutional modernity could come from nothing but anti-intellectualism.

But strictures there are. For it seems that in our day these supertheologians, often nonchurch in orientation and outlook, are the least criticized of the intelligentsia; teachers of the Christian masses, and well in advance of their time, they hold an enviable position. And in this country, traditional suspicion of intellectuals makes it foolhardy to express misgivings about popular theologians to the somewhat reluctant but supporting public. But the strictures may lead the way to integrity and honesty. The Christian cause may be served by intellectual scruples as well as by premature syntheses and plausible gambits.

Today we are living in a supposedly post-Christian world, bereft of God. Many people are assimilating Bonhoeffer's somewhat undeveloped thought about this as almost an axiom. Agreed, Bonhoeffer did have misgivings, which he shared with his correspondents (in *Letters and Papers from Prison*), about the traditional theistic intellectual apparatus by which God was described as "out there" and as merely a stopgap to account for that which science could not explain. But Bonhoeffer was remarkably subtle and was also a confirmed believer in Jesus Christ. His quarrel was with certain intellectual schemes which he had intimately shared and which he was progressively picking to pieces and discarding.

The end result of Bonhoeffer's thinking was not that modern conditions require Christians to be atheists. Certainly the statement that the idea of "God" and the word "God" are dead leads to difficulties. Bonhoeffer makes it explicit that the trouble arises from a kind of pervasive supernaturalistic and theological-technical use of the word "God." Though it has been accepted by most Christians, Bonhoeffer thought it could be abandoned without losing Jesus Christ and his significance. However, he seemed to think—and many of today's theologians seem to agree with him—that one would need still another scheme to give the word "God" some vitality.

II. THE IDEA OF GOD

It seems to be clear enough that there are no major commanding intellectual frames today in which the idea of God is necessary or even advantageous. Once it was different: the idea of "God" and surely the word "God" had a place in intellectual schemes associated with Aristotle, Plato, Whitehead, Kant, and others. No major metaphysical system of today seems widely compelling or even particularly useful. But the odd and unwarranted inferences which the modern theological set draw from this state of affairs, as set forth by Paul van Buren in his *The Secular Meaning of the Gospel* and John A. T. Robinson in his *Honest to God,* are truly surprising if not downright alarming.

Those inferences are that the Christian idea of God is dead and gone and that if Christians do not have a metaphysical scheme, they cannot use the word "God" as a name or believe "responsibly" that God exists. It is the latter inference that sustains the new interest in "ontology"—a science apparently calculated to make it convincing that God has being. Many contemporary theologians seem convinced that modern Christians must be a new

breed because they have been required to change their
metaphysical beliefs so drastically.

Tillich and others, making use of Ps. 139 and other *de
profundis* themes in Scripture, have tried to refurbish the
idea of "God" with notions of "ground" and "depth"
drawn from psychological sources, in place of "cause"
and "design" drawn from consideration of the world and
the cosmos. Ontological and existential theologians have
employed these themes in various ways in the endeavor
to warrant use of the word "God." But it is not necessary
for Christians to borrow the idea of God or even enlarge
it by such devices. There is a Christian way to get the
idea of God to work; one reaches it via one's need for
integrity and purity, one's sense of failure at self-perfec-
tion, one's continuing dismay with his faults—in short,
one's impotence, evil, and need. The elements of the
Christian's idea of God are thus achieved very slowly,
and the minimum means are the help of the Scripture and
a life of questing and continual striving.

Some may be dismayed by the fact that these means
are not made more openly apparent, but to do this would
encourage a kind of spiritual cheating. Furthermore, the
Christian idea of God has never been the coin of a very
large realm. What has passed for the idea of God, a currency that has been in relatively wide use, has usually
lacked the distinctive effects and uses that belong to the
Christian idea. It has been used to explain in a loose way
rather than to stir the sluggish human spirit. But this is
not to say that the idea of God is only an idea and
nothing more.

III. IRRELEVANT ARGUMENT

The other notion—that without a metaphysical scheme
the Christian idea of God is only subjective, has no refer-

ence, or is only an idea and not a name—is simply incorrect. Christians learn to use the word "God" just as we use most words, namely, referentially. And the ordinary ways of speaking and thinking have scarcely changed through the centuries. The special concepts and categories by which we describe new styles of thinking are irrelevant to the Christian use of the word "God." The word "God" is used with a meaning distinguished, of course, by the old Christian sources and practices but also in the same manner that we use most of our other words that name persons, places, and things. This way of using the word "God" requires that one dares all the conditions of faith, hope, and love, by virtue of which one becomes certain that God also loves and cares. Then, and only then, does it become "inconceivable" to say that God does not exist.

Doubt of God's existence is not assuaged by new metaphysical schemes. It takes courage to believe in a God who redeems and judges, cares and creates, and courage does not come by a fell swoop nor is it a by-product of confidence in some more encompassing scheme. Furthermore, it has not been shown that Christian belief comes more easily in times of flourishing metaphysical thought. The Christian belief in God can be understood and described only through a kind of thinking which has little or no historical background, little or no special technique, namely, our common sense. All of us, as a matter of common sense, come to believe in people, the world, and perhaps God. We have no special proof for existence, only very ordinary ways to come to the confidences by which we live. Our philosophizing and theologizing do not establish God's existence any more than natural science proves the existence of that which it describes. Learning to use the word "God" referentially does not come about through a special science; rather, it is both the sign of and consequence of faith.

IV. THE PRICE IS HIGH

It is also a theme of the *avant-garde* that the theology of the Christian church is outmoded, irrelevant, and an inducement to unbelief; the fault of the church lies in being withdrawn, "irrelevant," and unaware of science, industrialization, and contemporary man. So goes the new litany! Apparently a new theology is required for social relevance. Talk of the need for thought forms suitable to the age creates the impression that the apostles stated the kerygma in terms applicable to themselves and that recently churchmen have only reiterated these terms, forsaking the new, pertinent media.

This, too, is rubbish; theology never did have the allegiance of the intelligentsia in the West, nor did the church's other powers extend over the whole of European social life. The mercantile princes of Europe pursued money and pleasure in thoroughly pagan ways. Europe was "Christian" chiefly in the annals of Christian historians.

The church may lament the fact that the intellectuals are separated from it, but it is certainly not true that they were ever unanimously Christian. The depiction of faith in past ages is deceptive: it sustains the illusion that once theology was indubitable, compelling, and immediately relevant to all intelligent people, whereas today it is dubious, optional at best, and pertinent only to people who already believe on other than intellectual bases. Though one hesitates to recommend a radical intellectual scheme, it is nevertheless true that Christianity is still much the same old thing. The reason for theological change has never been the failure of language because of its limitations and its temporal nature but rather the varying conditions to which the faith is addressed. Therefore the theologian must understand the world and the people in it, not to make Christianity relevant to them as much as to help them become relevant and amenable to Christianity.

This complaint about the church's outmoded theology must not be taken lightly. It creates the conviction that the whole world would like to become Christian if only the theologians would become modern. Of course, the price is a little high: resurrection, atonement, the virgin birth, the last judgment, lately God and a few other things must go, but everything else, and especially the meaning of these, can be kept! Does not even Bultmann speak this way? This is what happens when the responsibility is laid unequivocally on the church and the theologians—the only possible way to make Christianity palatable is to strip everything from it and make its meanings coextensive with what people will discern for themselves and believe anyway.

V. OF SCIENCE AND SUNSETS

There is a third stricture: It is being continually asserted that the church and the theologians are not giving serious attention to science. But it cannot be said that Christian theology is the only or even a particularly strong support of obscurantism. That may have been true at one time or in a particular circumstance but it is not correct as a general statement. Most churchmen, including theologians, are aware of modern theories about the causes of events and behavior and can discuss them intelligibly, and they can take in their stride discoveries, explorations, and new hypotheses. And that they do this increasingly is well recognized.

The criticism, I take it, is posited upon the idea that every such accommodation to science and other new learning must entail a corresponding change in theology.

Somehow, somewhere, the understanding of the logical structure of theology has become so confused that it is assumed that changes in what we think of as the details of knowledge must imply a change in the outlook, that is, the theological view. Therefore, to accept new scientific explanations is thought to require a scientific philosophy of life or what one might call a scientific outlook. This is certainly random talk, but even Bultmann's discussions about demythologizing Scripture are as logically loose as one can imagine, though invariably to the effect that science makes even theological differences.

An example can show us how incorrect such an approach is. We have all been accustomed to talk, in a variety of ways, about the beauty of the sunrise and the sunset; those very words and concepts are as old as language itself. In the course of history we have learned much about the planets, the sun, and celestial motions. But to think that the language about sunrises and sunsets is less viable now because of our new knowledge of astronomy or that it is now only metaphorical instead of literal—that would be a real howler. Such an error would lie in confusing the two ways of talking and understanding, not in the actual use of them. Certainly the most learned astronomer never outgrows the need for talking about the sunrise and the sunset, and it is obtuse or dogmatic to hold that one outlook is more true than the other or is a function of it or even a metaphor for it.

Our inherited language about sunrises and sunsets will not be refined nor even replaced by scientific achievements. It still has a role even though it has never been the expression of a very precise kind of thinking. This is somewhat true of theology too. For when it is said that God made the world and Jesus is the Son of God, that language was never based on poorly developed science any more than it must now be revived by new science.

And it is by no means correct to say that Christians

therefore speak only in myths and metaphors, symbols and figures, while scientists speak literally and truthfully. If this were the case, science would indeed be the source and fountainhead of all responsible speech, and theology would be only a temporary medium of expression, useful perhaps for motivating behavior and stimulating feelings but for little else. But sunsets are beautiful; and if anyone doubts that—or questions whether a Copernican could talk about them—we must show him the sunset and bring him into the family of mankind that talks about it so effectively. So, too, it is with Christian theology, though the process is probably not quite so easy because the stakes are so much higher. After all, even the most glorious sunset does not compare with eternal salvation.

VI. REFASHION MEN, NOT THE FAITH

Perhaps it goes without saying, then, that many of these charges that the churches are solemn but noisy assemblies and the theologies are irrelevant tissues of outmoded discourse are themselves suspect. The matter goes even further, for Protestantism especially has no restraints against such attacks, and that is entirely to the good; and it is only by free discussion and continuing criticism that these issues will remain vital. But it is time that a strong stand be taken about this posture of the neo-Protestant intelligentsia—in order not to discourage the continuing work of the Protestant minister and the ongoing ministry of the church.

I do not champion the old in preference to the new, nor augment the glories of the Reformation at the expense of the twentieth century. But I do say that the kind of theology associated with the apostles, even with Luther, Calvin, Wesley, and many others, was not simply a product of reading nor a fruit of research. It had a touch of personal assimilation, arising from the fact that it grew out of a drama in which its scribe was also an actor, and God was the reputed playwright. The everlasting tinkering with the theologies, as if they were corrigible only by analogy with scientific hypotheses and political policies, maligns the faith itself. It is high time, therefore, to think harder about the faith in order to see why men believe at all.

It is not true, for example, that theology tells us what can be believed and what cannot. For theology was never so much a matter of evidence that it had to change as the evidence advanced. Therefore it is a mistake for the restless theological set to insist that the church be a power in world affairs or that the theology of the church be made easily acceptable. This is not an argument for quietism nor for stubborn nonpertinency. But it is to say that the church has to be true to its very peculiar role just as theology must be related first to the range of themes that make up the faith. Both church and theology are faced with the tedious task of refashioning men, one by one, and the world, rather than refashioning the faith—either its role or its teachings—to render it more plausible.

Gabriel Vahanian

SWALLOWED UP
BY
GODLESSNESS

NOW ON THE FIRST DAY of the week
Mary Magdalene came to the
tomb early, while it was still dark, and saw that the stone
had been taken away from the tomb. So she ran, and
went to Simon Peter and the other disciple, the one
whom Jesus loved, and said to them, 'They have taken
the Lord out of the tomb, and we do not know where
they have laid him.'" (John 20:1–2.)

It is evident that the "death of God" does not mean the
same thing to all those who have proclaimed it. From
Jean Paul and Nietzsche to Jean-Paul Sartre and the "new
atheists" one may also wonder, therefore, whether it is
the same God who has been so loudly autopsied. Even
so, none of this would be shocking if it were merely the
prelude to a new religion or to pure and unadulterated
godlessness. But some new atheists, whose system of
thought could appropriately be termed "atheosophy" or,
perhaps better, "Christosophy" (since they make it sound
more positive than negative), also profess to be Christian.

A contradiction in terms? No, if we listen to them and,
with them, remember in particular that the early Chris-

From *The Christian Century*, December 8, 1965. Copyright 1965
Christian Century Foundation. Reprinted by permission.

tians themselves were charged with atheism. In fact, the new atheists are so far from being able to see any contradiction between this so-called atheistic Christosophy and Christianity that one wonders on the one hand what has happened to the scandal and foolishness of the gospel and, on the other, whether this new step is not a part of the fatal acculturation in which Christianity has compromised itself but which these new atheists or Christosophists seem to denounce vehemently.

If the death of God has occurred—and indeed it has—it is not by capitulating to or by coming to terms with the resultant immanentist cultural frame of thought that Christianity is going to become relevant to our present situation, unless, of course, Christosophy is still fighting the old battle which was lost in the death of God. This is why the so-called Christosophical alternative to the fossil that Christianity has become—the flamboyant and fervent descriptions notwithstanding—either is merely the ultimate though opposite consecration of mystical rationalism or is the supreme though inverted rationalization of mystical deism.

Compound the absence or the remoteness of God as you will, the reality of godlessness as a possible authentic alternative to Christianity will not necessarily be seriously taken into account. On the contrary, the result can be only another self-explanatory system which, like all such systems, makes sense by ultimately bypassing the truth it intended to expound, namely, that of the gospel which puts all our self-verifying truths into question. In order for such systems to stand, either God must be invented if he does not exist or he must be killed if he does—and both concepts are deficient because they are both predicated on *something* which either is missing or is *de trop*. Certainly, we must correlate the gospel with the empirical, even atheistic, truths that modern man lives by. But do we need to confuse it with them, too?

I

It was bad enough to inherit a God-based concept which had lost all concrete meaning. It is incomparably worse to attenuate and in fact deny the reality of the death of God by sublimating it into a newfangled soteriological concept. The "death of God" makes sense and is indeed a liberating event only when it is considered as a cultural phenomenon. But to argue that a historical fact (personally I prefer to call it a cultural phenomenon) as such, in and of itself, totally and exclusively lays claim to my whole existence amounts to making it into a new absolute, an idol hailed at the front door with all the red carpet treatment while God is whisked out through the back door. Also, I do not see how, by turning a cultural event into an article of faith, such an attitude differs from the old *credo quia absurdum est.*

Indeed, which position is more radical: simply to hold that the death of God is the cultural event that definitely seals the transition from the Christian to the post-Christian era, or to turn it into some kind of necessary soteriological premise; to recognize that godlessness is today a valid alternative to faith in God precisely because it denies not only God but any other kind of universal hypothesis with its converse, one distilled from the death of God? Granted, the early Christians were called atheists. But that was because, rejecting the cult of the emperor, they would not surrender to the religious syncretism to which their contemporaries were addicted. And though they all had the same world view, the early Christians nonetheless considered the predominantly religious self-understanding of man as the sickness, not the remedy.

By contrast, it seems that this new Christosophy not only surrenders to the secularism of our time but views it as the remedy instead of the sickness. Not that Christianity must always systematically oppose the world and its wisdom. Rather, it cannot satisfy itself with them and rest in them if it must make them possible and honor them. That is why, in keeping with the gospel, I feel that the more secular theology is, the less it will be predicated on secularism, just as Paul's theology was not predicated on the religious exigencies of his listeners in whose vernacular he proclaimed the gospel. All of us, incidentally, would do well to ponder the experience of those who undertook the task of translating the Latin Mass into the vernacular only to discover that it became even more meaningless.

II

Once again: Which, I should like to ask, is more radical today: to let faith question and especially be itself questioned, or to be swallowed up by godlessness; to recognize that theology is vulnerable, or to erect it into a science unquestionably consistent with itself only because it has capitulated to the atheistic exigencies of a contemporary world view?

As the cultural phenomenon which has alienated us both religiously and culturally from the Biblical conception of God, the death of God is what prevents us—much more effectively than any atheosophy of any sermon—from putting our trust in religion and its paraphernalia or their substitute. It becomes the springboard for a new religiosity when it is transformed into an article of faith. Putting the gospel upside down or inside out results not in a religionless Christianity, much less in a godless Christianity, but in an ersatz which is not less religious for being godless. At least God talk has the merit of having once been relevant. And I do not see how the secularism of this new religiosity is going to be successful precisely where religion itself has failed. If from the

Biblical point of view it is not religion that saves, one can scarcely avoid realizing that it is not secularism, either.

The more I think about it, the more odd I find it that these new Christosophists, who began with the idea of a religionless Christianity or—its corollary—the seculariza-tion of Christianity, should end up with nothing more to offer than the same old opium. They do remind us, mean-while, that, statements to the contrary notwithstanding, Christianity, even if secularized and atheistic, will remain what it has always *also* been—religion; but with this dif-ference: that Biblical Christianity represents that reli-gious consciousness in which man is saved not by but in spite of, as well as from, his religiosity and its implicit if latent positivism (which is what I take it Feuerbach meant when he said that "atheism . . . is the secret of religion").

We must confess therefore that Bonhoeffer's proposal of a "religionless Christianity" though perhaps not ill founded has certainly been ill construed, if not by him at least by those who have developed it into what is in-deed its logical conclusion—a godless Christianity or, more exactly, a non-Christian religion. Feuerbach, when he reduced theology to mere anthropology, was at least more consistent than our Christosophists who evacuate all significance from the death of God and turn it into a hoax.

Indeed, to admit that the Biblical world view is no longer valid need not prevent our realizing that the reality of God was affirmed not because of but in spite of the world view, transcendental though it was, or sacral and all that; so that, though the Bible was written in terms of a given world view we can still claim that it neither has nor is a world view, and that consequently no world view, immanentist or otherwise, *ipso facto* in-validates theology or faith in God. As a matter of fact, an immanentist world view might yet help us to grasp and live more concretely the meaning of faith as eschatological existence: for the first time in twenty centuries, God is not a crutch, God is not "reasons."

There is another factor muddling the sane approach to the significance of the "death of God" as a cultural phenomenon and ultimately denying its reality. This factor has two aspects. The first concerns the deploration that because of the secularization of Christianity we have lost the sense of the sacred and the world itself has lost its sacred dimension. The second is actually the converse of the first; it consists of the positivistic contention that, if I may put it in an aphorism, the secular is the real and the real is the secular. To begin with, I should like to remark that what we are told in effect is either that Christianity makes sense only within the context of a certain world view—a sacral one—or that Christianity cannot make sense today unless, in accordance with our contemporary atheistic world view, we separate its original truth from the instrument that was once used to convey this truth.

III

These seemingly two contradictory aspects coalesce when we realize that a sacral conception of the universe need not be theistic and, on the other hand, that "God" had nothing to do with the truth that was conveyed, but was an element of or an adjunct to the vehicle of that truth and is therefore to be excised for the sake of preserving that truth. This may be so. But then we must be candid enough to admit either that this has nothing to do with the gospel or that we are back where we started from and it is time for us to recognize that the task is to write a new gospel, not to patch up the old one.

In offering an alternative to this dilemma, let me say first of all that Christianity did not secularize but *desacralized* the world. Secularization is a symptom of another phenomenon; i.e., loss of faith or the betrayal of faith by the very institutions and creeds and dogmas meant to incarnate or transmit it. But from the beginning, faith had to desacralize the world or to dedivinize nature if it really meant (as Bultmann puts it) to "give back to the world its authentic worldliness." That in this process Christianity itself was secularized and gave birth to secularism is obviously another problem. Faith calls for secularity; secularism is the condition that dissolves faith and that results from the separation of the secular from the religious, of man's involvement in the world from his commitment to God. Because God is the creator and because his creation is not divine, the Bible holds that true secularity is the only religious mode of being; and by not separating the secular from the religious, it also affirms, so to speak, that the secular is the real and the real is the religious. That is to say, the world is not divine but it is the theater of God's glory, and true secularity is as different from secularism as it is from pantheism. Nor would I, in this light, be unwilling to contend that, *mutatis mutandis,* though the church, its creeds, and practices have become outmoded in the main they were once the means by which the secular was affirmed.

I would conclude by saying that from the Biblical point of view the demarcation line is not between the sacred and the profane or between the religious and the secular—let alone between one world view and another and much less, accordingly, between theism and atheism (as I have tried to show in *Wait Without Idols*). The line is drawn between God and the idol, the creator and the creature. It is drawn between iconoclasm and idolatry, and no world view—atheistic or theistic—can prevent either self-deification or God's becoming the idol from which man is constantly to be set free in order to become that which he is not; namely, himself rather than God.

W. M. Alexander

DEATH OF GOD
OR
GOD OF DEATH?

THE PRINCIPAL WEAKNESS of the new radical theology propounding the "death of God" is that it is not radical enough. This is strange in view of the fact that radical honesty and honest radicality seem to be at one and the same time the most appealing and the most irritating features of a new way of thinking on the American scene.

There is an almost neurotic and certainly a desperate need in all quarters to prove that the representatives of this theology are illogical, or that they use language carelessly, or that it has all been thought of before, or that they are entitled to say anything they want to except to call themselves Christian, and so on. It's as though these men had exposed a secret about American religion which nobody playing the game was supposed to mention. Only a *faux pas* as radical as this could explain the hysterical reaction by nationally prominent preachers and the snide and condescending admonitions of the theological establishment.

The outbreak of criticism or even the rejection of a new idea is not of great significance; we may expect it.

From *The Christian Century*, March 23, 1966. Copyright 1966 Christian Century Foundation. Reprinted by permission.

The significant question concerns the reasons advanced. For the most part, the objections to the "death of God" theology are trivial. It simply is not a serious objection to point out that these thinkers are not Christians in the good old sense of the word. Nor is it a serious objection to claim that some of the metaphors employed in their thought are sensational but obscure and that the whole cloudy business could be penetrated by a sustained effort at semantic clarification.

Again, it is hardly a serious objection to grant the point that an existentialist preoccupation with meaninglessness and nothingness is certainly characteristic of our time, and to argue in effect that since this negativeness leads nowhere and since we are given a positive alternative to nothingness in the Word of God, no positive-thinking Christian would hesitate between these alternatives. Nor is it a serious objection to point out that since the *traditional* concept of God as immortal excludes mortality by definition, the "death of God" school is talking not about God but about some object of their own or others' imaginations. Likewise, it is not a serious objection to argue that though the dying of God in our culture has been courageously analyzed and evaluated by these new thinkers, they should have cried not cheered, deplored not exulted in, the phenomenon. Other objections—such as that more people believe in God now than ever before, or that God is inscribed on our currency, and so on—are even more trivial and need not consume our attention.

These are not serious objections because they are beside the point. None is relevant to the position that the life and death of God is a historical event. History is much too serious a matter for us to nurse the fiction that the death of God is simply a strange metaphor, an odd way of talking about something that in itself is unquestioned—as though the substantialist metaphysics of these critics of the "death of God" school remains quite intact and unquestioned, as though Feuerbach, Dilthey, and Nietzsche never happened.

The "death of God" theologians are sanguine in regard to, if not proud of, their claim to radicality. But it ought to be noticed that for several reasons their radicality is hardly more than a claim. They are radical in that they are introducing a way of thought new to America, but not radical enough in that in it they are failing to challenge illusions peculiar to American thought. They are radical in attacking one version of middle-class faith, but not radical enough to launch an attack on a much more firmly entrenched pagan mythology now adapted to the American scene. They are radical in calling to the attention of Americans—not just existentialists—the phenomenon of meaninglessness, but they are not challenging the unoriginal and facile interpretation of this meaninglessness. They are radical in calling for a criticism of Christian tradition, but hardly radical in that they fail to question the absolutizing of the present. They are radical in their vision associating God with death, but uncritical of their presuppositions which force them to impose a Pelagian metaphysics upon their vision.

I. Myths Mutually Reinforced

Announcement of the "death of God" is not a new phenomenon, but it is new to the popular culture of the United States. Unfortunately its appearance on the American scene occurred in a context in which the new religious myth of the "death of God" and the old American myth of national identity coincide and mutually reinforce one another, a context in which particular American illusions and pretensions can be maintained. As the New Eden risen out of the ruins of an old dying world, as the New Creation and New Birth made possible by the death of an effete and outmoded European parentage, North

America has encouraged in her sons a belief in the illusion that they have escaped the prejudices and limitations of their past and are not subject to the historical limitations of the culture they left behind.

In the same connection, it is still an American dogma that history has not essentially affected this nation—or if it has, it has been a history which we have ourselves created *de novo*. So at one and the same time we can be contemptuous of history, can rejoice in death as the clearing away of obstacles to progress, can apotheosize our present activity and plans. For these reasons a new mythology which announces a negation of the past and the possibility of a civilizing and humane future does not constitute a radical attack on our American faith.

The early Christian gospel came as a radical attack on the culture of its age; the wrath of God was a symbol for the inescapable judgment on human activity and pretension; God appeared in terms of penultimate, even ultimate, death. The new American gospel comes as a palliative justification of national illusions, so that it is now possible to find *religious* support for our oldest national mythology. Now we can redefine God in the American image for the purpose either of rejecting or accepting him as it suits us, can judge judgment itself, can discover a cosmic buttress for our self-esteem.

II. Too Radical for Acceptance

The message that God is dead is a comforting message; it is a message for an affluent society, whether an affluent Jerusalem (which was addressed by its own prophets of the death of Yahweh), or an affluent Rome (which had its own apologists for the pagan mythologies of the dying gods Osiris, Mithra, Dionysus, and others), or an affluent America ready to hear the same message.

At some time or other the price must be paid for repudiating the insight of a Yahwist that atheism ("hardness of heart") is an act of God, the insight of a Second Isaiah that God does evil, the insight of a Hosea that God comes to Israel in terms of destruction and death, and that what we call the absence of God is as much the work of God as his presence.

The radical message is the prophetic message that God is not only life but death. This is the threat which the American will not accept, which he insists on overlaying with a new optimism and a new mythology. This is the threat that the death of God (the deathly form of his judgment) poses for the American Christian, the American middle-class church, the American dreams and plans, the American nation. As a nation we are now beginning to be introduced by Vietnam to the suspicion that we are not almighty, that our ultimate destiny as a nation might be death. And this suspicion will be re-inforced by fresh evidence from other "Vietnams" to come. Confronted by the possibility of the death of God in the radical sense (that is, the possibility that God will manifest himself as death), for us to say that "God is dead" is to indulge in the optimism of a false hope and a sentimental religion. That is so because the judgment of a God who is dead can be avoided and his death sur-mounted, while the death of *God* (subjective genitive) cannot be escaped.

This arresting metaphor of Nietzsche—"the death of God"—is more than a reaffirmation of the crucifixion of the God-man, although in the death of Jesus as the in-carnation of God both the death of God and the God of death ("My God, my God, why hast thou forsaken me?") are mysteriously united in one event. It is more than speech about the death of Christ, for in its recent usage the metaphor draws its significance from a pagan, myth-ological interpretation of history. God dies, but his is a mythical death. It occurs in a historical cycle. Faith is the vision of this process.

No radical attack on this mythological faith is allowed because this faith is the foundation of a scheme which gives meaning to the death of God as a historical event. The assumption behind the scheme which gives import and content to the metaphor is the basically pagan assumption that the gods are part of the cosmos—or, to put it another way, that the gods, whether Titans or Olympians or creations with Western Christian coloring, are subject to a destiny structured according to periods. Thus the death of God is "programmed," and this death is subject not only to destiny, which is the real ultimate, but in a sense also to man.

III. Presuppositions Get in the Way

This scheme, this periodization of history which calls to mind the historical philosophy of Joachim of Floris, can be grasped in mythical and apocalyptic form by the human mind. Thus man is superior to God, both in his knowledge of the scheme and in his surviving the "death of God." The radical theology of the death of God turns out to be a colossal self-deception: colossal because the scope is enormous—no less than an interpretation of all of history is attempted; self-deceptive because it has escaped notice that man in his ego has formulated a predicament which appears to be realistic and serious and which has many of the lineaments and dimensions of the seriousness of life, but which ultimately is no threat to man himself. It enables man to sacrifice God without getting hurt.

It is possible for gods to die if they are fortunate enough to be born in the matrix of a chronological process, which then is the real ultimate. To express the same myth in a different form: if what is ultimate is a historical modalism—whether Sabellian or Joachimite or Marxist or "radical Christian"—then it is possible to say that "God is dead." But under such circumstances man has no chance of being faced with any reality so radical as a judgment in which death is an ultimate. The presuppositions of this mythology which prevents the theologian from seeing the phenomenon of guilt, anxiety, meaninglessness, and death in the sense of the "death of God," the wrath of God, and the judgment of God rather than in a topsy-turvy, anthropomorphic sense—those presuppositions need to be subjected to intense and radical criticism.

The presuppositions include the liberal beliefs of optimism, nourished by U.S. affluence and power, as well as an unexamined Pelagianism, which begins by taking the wrath of God in a truncated and disjunctive sense and ends by understanding the "death of God" in the same sense. It was Pelagius who understood the sin of man and the wrath of God in an individualistic and atomistic manner. If wrath, judgment, and death continue to be understood in this sense, not as the presence of God in a total cultural and cosmic sense, is it possible for the presence of God as life, love, and grace to be understood in the same truly radical sense?

Selected Correspondence:
The Response
of the Public at Large

Edited by Jackson Lee Ice

LETTERS TO WILLIAM HAMILTON

Professor hamilton's suggestive observation that "today's theology is being written in letters" may be more astute than one realizes at first. Its plausibility impressed us more and more as we read through the personal correspondence of both Professor Altizer and Professor Hamilton. It was a coveted experience. We learned more not only about the men but also about the stirrings of a new movement and the feelings and impressions of the people who shared it with them. We were struck by the fact that too often the important contributions which these interpersonal dialogues make to the total community of thought is underestimated: not only the encouragement and support which they give, but also the needed criticisms, sober reminders, and invaluable suggestions. We cannot judge what all the religious leaders and laymen of the country are writing to each other today, but if what we have read in connection with this debate is any indication, we would say that the amount of intelligent searching and profound discussion going on among theologians, clergy, and laymen via the mail is greater than one realizes. This cultural factor ought to be taken into account in understanding the full effect and implications of any new movement of thought. Certainly there is a different *kind* of theological writing here, but that it is genuine and vital, we have no doubt.

This, we are sure, is what Professor Hamilton has in mind. It is the kind of intensely personal radically open exchange which he feels is integral to the development of living patterns of religious thought. Its roots are where they should be—deep in the milieu of actual changing situations and human needs. It serves as a sounding board and allows a kind of auscultation necessary for an innovator to keep his ideas alive. In the privacy of a letter the priest and minister, the student and housewife —if they feel a kinship with someone who will listen— can drop their theological vestments for a time and freely speak about religious questions which knock bothersomely on the backs of their minds. Many do so with sighs of relief and complete candor, especially if the questions have been habitually repressed by social censor or ecclesiastical taboo. Such discussions are refreshingly to the point, often caustic or witty, but in the main deadly serious. There is also a more sanguine sharing of biases and blind spots, and, for some, the cathartic experience of being able to laugh openly at themselves and their religious postures. Through them all, one feels the thrust of their private feelings and the urgency of their questions. Usually devoid of academic terminology, these groping expressions are unsystematic and at times inchoate, but what they lose in scholarly acumen, they gain in directness and fervor. Here one may read the unexpurgated confessions of contemporary man's faiths and doubts. Perhaps the deep diapasons of a future theology are already being sounded in such correspondence.

The following letters, selected from the surprising deluge of mail that Professor Hamilton received as the result of the controversy, come from people of diverse interests and backgrounds. As one would imagine, their reactions run the gamut from violent opposition to patronizing support.

For example, there were several sympathy cards with brief comments attached, some facetious ("I heard that you have lost a dear friend"), some sincere ("Deepest sympathy, for you are really without hope. Your God is dead. Mine lives. He truly lives!"). There were the to-be-expected unsigned hate letters ("You dirty commie atheist homosexual bastard!"), and the fanatical defenders of God-and-Country letters ("You are a Communist working in the international conspiracy against Jesus Christ and Christians. . . . Do you think you are fooling Jesus Christ and don't you think you will be severely punished for being such a heretic? But in your state of mind, who can reach you? Maybe you are beyond hope, but that you should destroy young people's minds with your insane drivel should make true Christians want to kick you right out of the U.S.!"). And there were the condescending we-knew-it-all-the-time letters ("It's about time you theologians saw the truth"). But these responses were in the minority.

On the whole, the letters were sane and serious. This is not to imply that they were all in agreement—some were generally favorable, many were strongly critical. Some, for instance, felt that Professor Hamilton had gone too far ("I fail to see how you can deny the Deity of Christ and still remain a Christian"), some that he had not gone far enough ("Why Jesus? Why not go all the way and become a humanist?"). But such statements reflect concerned and responsible critics. It is interesting that even a large number of those who were opposed to Hamilton felt his disarming honesty and expressed gratification that he had said what he did. They voiced interest that at least something new was stirring and welcomed the challenge.

Take, for example, this letter from a Catholic sister

teaching in a parochial high school:

Dear Dr. Hamilton:

Since, as any sincere innovator, you have undoubtedly been receiving many letters of disapproval, I hope that it may be of some small comfort to you to know that there are those of us who recognize the contributions you have made to religious and Christian thinking. Although I cannot honestly subscribe to some of your conclusions, I appreciate the awareness which you have given me—the awareness of the lack of relevance which religion has in the minds of my students, and of the inadequacies of my own attempts to make religion meaningful to them. You are in the goodwill and prayers of one who believes in your good faith and intellectual honesty.

Here's one from a Baptist minister who is more intrigued than alienated:

Dear Dr. Hamilton:

I thank you for your latest public statement as it appeared in *Christianity and Crisis*. I haven't the foggiest notion of what you are saying so long as you retain the name Christian, but I have no desire to patronize or dismiss you. The rest of the article, your other writing, and your reputation as a theologian in general all keep me listening and reading. I suspect that I shall only be kept awake and growing by people like yourself. I hope you will continue to write. I hope I am wrong in detecting, in some of your writing, an individualism, or privatism, which could lead you off into a corner.

Though strangers, I wish you a very meaningful Christmas.

And in the same vein a Congregational minister wrote:

Dear Dr. Hamilton:

Thank you for the article "The Shape of a Radical Theology," *The Christian Century,* October 6.

I now plan to read "The New Essence of Christianity" and your next book.

I think I shall disagree, but as with a very admirable opponent. You are serving us either as a founder of thought or as an excellent challenger.

Typical of so many of the favorable letters that Hamilton received are the following. The majority of these came, not as responses to the magazine or newspaper editorials, but, which is not surprising, from a reading of his own articles that appeared in the leading journals. The first is from a woman who was enthusiastic over being able, as a layman, to understand and participate in a theologian's ideas which she found most enlightening:

For the first time in all the years I've been reading *The Christian Century* I can't refrain from writing an author. Your article in the October 6 issue thrilled me. You talk religion to me and sensible revolt. You share the controversy. *Now* if you and the like-minded ones can put into laymen's English what you are thinking and believing and arguing about, perhaps we poor, ignorant laymen can get a peek at theology. Perhaps you can even share the adventure. Most of us in this day and age aren't looking for religion "once and for all delivered" and can be trusted to understand that the clergy can believe one thing this year and unthink it next year. Sharing your uncertainties may make some would-be Christians respect you more. Oh, I know it is risky. I hear church people talk. But if the church is to get the respect and attention it craves it may have to risk even in theology as they are risking in social

ventures. I do hope the projected (?) new journal
will keep us in mind.

Honest to God has opened the floodgates for laymen.
When I asked a minister friend what he thought of the
book he replied that these ideas were discussed and
largely accepted in his seminary forty years ago. Wonderful. But why, oh why, hasn't more trickled down to
the churchgoer? I can guess some of the answer, and
it is no great credit to the seminaries or the clergy.
Some of it, for my money, can be blamed on the
esoteric language and Germanic lingo which has discouraged us.

Bravo!!! I understood every word of your article.

A Presbyterian minister spoke of specific help he received:

I have just finished reading your article in the latest
Christian Century, "The Shape of a Radical Theology."
I am deeply grateful for it. I have recently had some
copies made to send to friends with whom I am in
dialogue concerning this type of theology.

You put into words what I discover I believe and
you do it so clearly that I can say to others, this is what
I believe but have not been able to formulate adequately. As a minister in the Presbyterian Church U.S.,
one can imagine the difficulty of the situation in which
I find myself. But I have not been able to begin to
deal with the situation because all of my formulations
have been dominated with a negative tone. With your
statement I can begin on a positive note.

A professor of applied theology wrote:

I have just read your article on "The Shape of a
Radical Theology" in the current *Christian Century*.

I feel as I imagine a man would feel who had been scrounging around for years in a dark room searching for the light switch or matches for a kerosene lamp or even a half-burned-out candle, and accidentally releases the blackout blind over the room's one window and is suddenly shattered by the warming, illuminating, penetrating midday sun!

Words, especially written ones, are such puny and wholly inadequate vehicles for the expression of true emotion. It is so far short of what I really feel merely to say "Thank you," but I do say it from the pit of my stomach and with genuine sincerity.

I dislike tags—ecclesiastical, theological, or otherwise. They seem to me to be often cruel and always inaccurate. In terms of your article, however, I would have to confess to being *both* a "soft" and a "hard" theological radical. I have deep, bone-aching difficulty with "the message" (and my years at good old Union Theological Seminary did not do anything to clarify the difficulty). But I am equally concerned about the communication of the message. When and if I get my mind made up about the message, I simply can't sit and congratulate myself: there must be a proclamation, a communication, a declaration—not only of the fact that the blackout blind can actually be released, but some indication of how one can arrive at the location of the blind without spending most of his life and taking all of the skin off his shins bumping and falling around in the search for it.

As one out here who mourns, but who in all honesty has been forced to acknowledge, the "death of God," I covet the fellowship of those who are in the search, and would appreciate knowing of the time and place of their getting together of which you speak.

Congratulations upon turning forty and coming of age! I am aware experientially of the joys and the freedom which this middle-age divide in one's life brings, as well as the added difficulties and challenges it makes possible.

A disenchanted chaplain of a state college wrote:

> I read your *Theology Today* article, "Thursday's Child," a few days after trying, with a resident neurosurgeon . . . to get a family to allow an operation on their father. There was a tumor on his brain and there was a good 50-50 chance that it was benign. The family's only response, to me and to the doctor, was, "It is God's will that it is Daddy's time to go." For me that day God crumbled out of the cracks of existence. And since that day I have had to ask about the meaning of Jesus. I found that I am in general agreement with you and others who are asking these same questions.

A voice from the South:

> In answer to your question, I want to say: Yes, there are some of us "out here" who have had the same kind of experience which you describe. In fact, there may be more of us than you might believe.
> As both an active pastor and a graduate student in counseling psychology, I have increasingly become disenchanted with the role of the church in the modern community, and have grappled mightily with the problems which "middle-of-the-road, ecumenical orthodoxy" has presented me. And like yourself, it was Bonhoeffer who began to stir up the seeds of discontent within my own little, comfortable theological rationale.
> I am not yet completely sure just what kind of a radical I am becoming. I have gone through the "soft

radical" stage—and have found it wanting. So I suppose I am well on the road to becoming a "hard" one.
You are quite correct in saying that our problem is not
one of communication—but rather the content of what
we attempt to say. I am completely discouraged with
the trend toward using the faith as one among many
ways to solve man's living problems. Rather than a
vehicle for giving security in an otherwise insecure
world, cannot the faith through radical obedience to
Jesus prepare us to live creatively and freely in spite
of our insecurities? Cannot the church say to the world
that through this radical obedience man can, and must,
work himself out of his corporate and individual predicament, without depending on God who will "bail us
out" of our plight? Is this what the new radical theology is trying to say? If so, then count me in.

A minister of a Congregational church in New England "reluctantly" comes to a "painful" conclusion:

I am becoming increasingly interested in the thinking that underlies the "death of God" theology. After
fifteen years' experience in the parish ministry I am
forced to conclude—albeit rather reluctantly—that a
painful truth is expressed in the "God is dead" concept.
I do not have secular man in mind; from my observation I have found that God is only a nebulous idea for
many people within the church. At best he is but an
abstraction from which most of the meaning has been
squeezed out. He seems to be totally irrelevant (isn't
this the fashionable word?) in the daily grind. If he
functions at all, it is as a sort of prop or crutch for
emergency purposes only. But even this must be questioned for its authenticity, for after the crisis has
passed, the crutch is discarded. Perhaps this is the fault
of us preachers—is it the old problem of failure of
communication again?

Many, knowing the harsh criticism and personal pressures which he had to endure, sent their encouragements, as did this medical doctor:

You have been in my thoughts in recent weeks as the winds blow about you. It's magnificent to see someone deeply engaged in the fundamental things that matter to people, and the ferment of your engagements is so needed in our times. Fools who don't understand what you're doing will shout "Heresy" and want your scalp, and some of these I suspect might even be among your board. But what you are doing is so necessary to the vitality of our whole society. You have my love and support. All the best to you.

Not all were so sympathetic. The notoriety that Hamilton's radical ideas suddenly attained threw an unexpected spotlight of public attention on the seminary where he taught—much to its embarrassment. It received numerous letters and phone calls from perplexed and angry people demanding to know what was going on. Obliged to make some statement of clarification, President Gene E. Bartlett announced: "We do not accept his views. We debate them and affirm the opposite. . . . His views do not represent Colgate Rochester Divinity School. Dr. Hamilton is the only one among us who holds that position." Though President Bartlett defended Hamilton's right to dissent and to continue teaching, Hamilton was asked "by mutual consent" to cease teaching his basic course in theology. Apparently he became something of a religious anomaly even among his own colleagues.

The result of the school's official attitude brought a swift and blunt response from some of its alumni. Their protest was not so much an endorsement of Hamilton's views as an expression of disappointment that his own, supposedly "liberal" seminary should abandon him at a time when he most needed and deserved its support. They also castigated the school for not recognizing the value of such religious ferment generated by one of its most challenging professors.

Here is an example of one of those letters addressed to President Bartlett with copies sent to several of the professors, as well as to Professor Hamilton:

I have been heartsick since I received the 1965 No. 2 CRDS Bulletin. I must likewise have made up more than a dozen letters to you in my mind. In fact, I have successively discarded one brilliant—snide—humorous —sarcastic—letter after another.

I presume that all people who are responsible tend to listen more to vocal criticism and are willing to note letters of dissent more so than the nonreceived letters of agreement. It strikes me that the "Big Debate" article is the standard reaction of any institution which finds itself in the uncomfortable position of being in the midst of relevant issues. Through the unexpected and unimagined horror of discovering a genius in its midst.

Why am I heartsick? Simply, that I was proud of CRDS, my school and my dad's school, perhaps someday my son's school. However, what was vaguely disturbing to me has now become clear, the old free tradition from Beaven through Saunders has drawn to a close irrevocably, and that, sir, is a real shame.

The public abandonment of a faculty member may or may not be in the school's interest—only you would know this. However, it is, regardless of issue, chickenlivered.

The work of van Buren, Cox, Hamilton, and Bishop Robinson has given campus clergy more opportunities for faculty discussion, and for graduate student questioning. The past two years have been exciting and worthwhile because of the pioneer work of these men, and has and will continue to enhance the image of the institutional church in the world. The people who are disturbed over the issues brought forth by these authors are the pastors who forget their Nietzsche, Kierkegaard, and other nineteenth- and twentieth-century authors. I find the work of all these men meaningful, and am quite sorry over the fear and trembling of those who read only doom into what is no more and no less a refreshing interlude in the life of the church.

I am sorry to cause you discomfort by this letter. However, that article is nothing to be proud of.

Here is the opinion of an editor of a Protestant religious journal, who wrote about Hamilton's unique role as a Christian theologian trying to involve himself in a meaningful dialogue with the secular world:

Lounge Car, New York Central Railroad, Outbound Rochester to New York—Bill, it was great to meet you and your wife this evening.

You asked me about "journalism," and "being publicized," and all that. Now let me look at this for a minute.

If you deliberately seek publicity, or try to gear your writing or ideas to what is "popular" or "acceptable," then you are a promoter and should seek this career. *But,* you don't seem to be this sort of person at all. You seem to be a Christian theological scholar who happens to find himself publicized—as a result of discovering and hewing to a position that is publicly exciting: i.e., relevant to the masses.

Therefore, the name of the game for you is *dialogue*. The posture is *involvement*. The daily fact is: *the reaction is the story,* and *the situation is open-ended.*

Your academic place is essentially that of Martin Luther. You are committed to affirming and discussing a position in the Christian tradition. This position brings you into sharp conflict with the priestly hierarchy of the time. And this conflict heats up and spreads the discussion. Luther used the major medium of *his* time: the academic debate. You have found yourself in the major medium of *our* time: the mass media of publishing and electronics. What has changed is not the basic role of the Christian scholar, but rather the media.

Involvement means entering into dialogue in the media of your time. For scholars, this has traditionally been a hangup. In Luther's time, the priestly scholars said in effect: "But, we don't mean that debate should be this *debatable*." There are doubtless others, unrecorded, who quietly rejected the cloister for the world. Luther's genius was to choose neither alternative, but rather to affirm Christian involvement as dialogue in the media of his time. As a result of priestly hostility, he reshaped man's relation to the media. He nailed his theses on the door, and thus reasserted the principle of publicly communicating the ideas of the Christian scholar. The same thing pertains in our time. Many Christian scholars say in effect: "But, involvement isn't that *involved*." Others, such as a friend I spoke about or a Charles Van Doren, capitulate to the media and abandon the role of scholar.

I'm not urging you to seek attention. But it is coming your way, and I'm suggesting that the media of our time, when properly approached by the scholar, may offer him a viable and possibly creative alternative to cloistered debate.

However, others were concerned about the implications of Hamilton's theology for the parish ministry and wondered what the role of the "new" theology could possibly be in the everyday life of the church. Here is a letter from a well-known New York City minister who expressed this concern:

Would you be good enough to help clarify my thinking with reference to the application of your theology to situational personal problems. I apologize for asking your indulgence, as I can well imagine how terribly busy you are. However, I feel the need of suggestions for carrying on my daily work with people in the light of the new theological ideas advanced by you and other distinguished thinkers.

There is always, I presume, a gap between the creative theological thinker and the practical responsibilities of a pastor. And my questions arise from the never-ending crises faced daily by plain people for whom the speculative work of scholars seems far removed, though in time it will, of course, filter down and recondition their present faith in God.

What would you suggest that I as a working pastor say to a mother and father whose five small children were burned or suffocated to death in a fire which destroyed their home a few days ago, without employing "God talk," and on the basis of the "God is dead" theology? How would you suggest going about my job of attempting to console and strengthen these bereaved parents? Also, what would be a procedure designed to give them adequate understanding of their problem?

Another case I face deals with an alcoholic who, as a result of his drinking problem, lost his job and was finally self-committed to a state institution for the treatment of alcoholism. A man of excellent education and extraordinary ability, and certainly no religious fundamentalist, he took to reading the Bible and, as he put it, "God saved me and removed the insatiable desire for alcohol." He became completely restored to constructive living. Reading of your "death of God" theology, he now asks me, to use his vernacular, "Am I kidding myself in believing that God had anything to do with my change, since he doesn't exist; if he doesn't exist, then just what did change me? And furthermore, if we have no God, what the hell difference does it make if one remains a drunk?"

This man wants an answer; in fact, he insists upon one, and frankly I am not able to give him an adequate explanation, not being myself too well versed in the new concept. What would you suggest that I tell him?

In these questions, which are typical of a minister's regular pastoral experience, I believe that I am raising a possible variance between a scholar's theology and a practical working pastor's methodology. I am seeking a significant way to relate one to the other.

This letter represents a sincere request for guidance in the sudden and developing new situation of working without the old God and Christ system of thought and practice. I shall be grateful for your advice and counsel.

A layman wrote about how Hamilton's ideas directly aided him in a time of personal need:

> I have read your book *The New Essence of Christianity*. . . . Your book made Christianity intellectually acceptable to me, and I have come to understand and love Christ to an extent I never believed possible. I shall always be grateful to you. If one of your goals as a Christian is to help others, you have at least one success to your credit.

A former minister, now an English teacher, whose interest in religion was reawakened by the new ferment, wrote:

The great bulk of current theology either irritates me because of its pompousness and stuffiness, or it leaves me with feelings of yawning indifference. So much of the traditional dogma that is ladled out in churches across the land strikes me as being dishonest, puzzling, dull, or simply irrelevant to our present needs. I therefore welcome your criticism of the orthodox approach. Indeed, I find the brief summary of your views presented by the magazine to be quite exciting. My interest has been whetted, and I am eager to read more of your arguments and proposals.

For your information, I was graduated from a theological seminary and served for ten years as a minister. Finally, in 1958, because I felt a deepening conflict between the official dogmas and pronouncements of my denomination and my personal beliefs and inclinations, I withdrew from the ministry. I did editorial work for five years and I'm currently teaching English.

In closing, let me add that this brief article has reawakened my interest in religion. Actually, it's still the field which fascinates me most, since it deals with what I consider to be the basic questions of human existence. It may well be that, after reading your works (as well as those of Professor Altizer and the others mentioned by *Time*), I'll want to take graduate work in religion and look for a post in college teaching.

Later, he commented, after reading the articles that Hamilton had sent him:

I've read your article several times, and I'm still ruminating its principal ideas and trying to understand its major implications. My initial reaction is something like this: I'm wholly in sympathy with your declaration that God is dead. If I were to express my own deepest feelings on the subject, I couldn't do better than to borrow your own straightforward expression: "It is really that we do not know, do not adore, do not possess, do not believe in God." And (very appropriately)—"We are not talking about the absence of the experience of God, but about *the experience of the absence of God.*" Not only am I in accord with this viewpoint, but I admire the courage and integrity which you display in expressing it publicly. My own training, at home and in the seminary, conditioned me to take a somewhat more cautious (and dishonest) approach as a minister. In effect, our seminary professors advised us "not to preach our doubts." The prevailing theory was that the average parishioner was fairly contented with the body of orthodox dogma, and the minister, whatever his personal attitudes (particularly his reservations and doubts) might be, should try to toe the "party line" in his public pronouncements. He should always speak the truth "in love." This meant, in effect, that he shouldn't rock the boat of comfortable tradition and superstition. As I look back on those days of my split theological personality, I'm sure that one or two professors of your caliber would have made a great difference in the way I handled this oppressive dilemma. I think that I too would have had the courage to stand up and be counted. I wouldn't have spent so much effort trying to nurse dead myths to life again, I wouldn't have wasted so much energy trying to submerge doubts that seemed to have more life in them than the proverbial cat. Freed from this seminary-inspired double-talk and hypocrisy, I might have invested a lot more time and energy in the more profitable business of following Jesus. I might even have persuaded a few of my parishioners to do likewise!

Actually, I suppose I shouldn't feel too uncharitable

toward professors who advised the charitable mouthing
of ancient platitudes and myths—nor toward myself
for following their advice. It just wasn't fashionable in
the Age of Faith twenty years ago to spout heresies
from the pulpit. Or, at least it wasn't considered good
pulpit form by the ministers whom I was associated
with.

To get back to your article. Your announcement of
the death of God has far-reaching implications. I've
only begun to suspect what they might be. Obviously,
if a Christian accepts your basic premises, he'll have
to do some drastic revising of his position on such
major questions as (1) the nature and function of the
church, (2) the place of Jesus in history, (3) the authority (if any) and appeal of Jesus for a modern
Christian, (4) the value for us of the Bible, of the
Christian creeds, and of the writings of major churchmen and theologians of the past, etc., etc.

Although you state emphatically that the chief vocation of a Christian is to move out from the altar into
the world and there to seek Jesus, to stay with him
and to do his work, you do not spell out many of the
other implications which your position certainly must
have for theology and for the church. (Indeed, what
does theology now become if the "theo" is removed?
Is it nothing more than a kind of pious psychoanalysis
in which no-god-ologians try to analyze and account
for the persistent illusions which men have had about
some nebulous being whom they called God?) These
questions do not imply an unfavorable criticism of the
article. I'd suspect that, at the time of writing, even
you hadn't worked out all the implications in detail;
or even if you had, space didn't permit you to explain
them. Indeed, I'd further guess that if the "God is
dead" movement displays considerable vitality and
growth—i.e., if it eventually enjoys a sympathetic re-

ception by large numbers of churchmen, scholars, and laymen—it will require the efforts of many people to fully work out the "implications" that I'm talking about. If a point of view like this really "catches on," the effects will surely be revolutionary. And in this, as in any revolution, the initial handful of radicals who denounce the old ways and point to the new cannot even dream of all the innovations that their ideas will produce in the thought and institutions of their generation.

A dissatisfied minister shares a typical dilemma characteristic of so many letters from the parish. He wrote:

> I want you to know that I was delighted with "Thursday's Child." It's a joy to find an intelligible statement of a theological proposition, in contrast to the verbose gibberish which has been dispensed by certain obscurantist theologians in recent years. I have come only lately on the scene of the radical theology of which you are a most eloquent spokesman. . . . Your writing strikes a responsive chord in me, who for so long have been floundering in the Stygian darkness of Barthianism. I am enchanted by the exciting new horizons which have been opened up. Your article in *The Christian Scholar* is meaty in content and the digestive process will be a lengthy one for me.
>
> As you may have surmised, I am disgruntled about the parish ministry—a not uncommon malady among ministers today. I am tempted to leave it. . . . If only some popular magazine would pay me a couple of thousand dollars to write an article about Why I Quit! Anyway, I may be forcibly relieved of my present post shortly. . . . I have had a few sermons on the new theology, attempting to analyze it by showing the religious situation which gave rise to it. Naturally this

has alarmed certain members of the congregation, especially those who didn't know what it meant when God was alive, but are highly indignant to hear of his death.

The trouble is . . . having given the worst years of my life to the ministry, I haven't the slightest idea what I'd do if I left it, and I am one of those unfortunate people who must work for a living. I am hopeful that Satan may come through with an attractive offer, though I'm wondering if he is still around—didn't he automatically accompany God into extinction? I've always suspected that he was secretly God's alter ego.

Well, perhaps I should don the mask of piety again (one of the guises of which you speak in "Thursday's Child"). Piety has never been my strong suit, but I can adjust the pious mask to suit the circumstances. . . . I've learned how to live as a hypocrite. . . . That's another lesson the parish ministry has taught me.

I have slogged through many a theological morass on my journey into (and out of) faith. The hopeful thing is that I have pulled through fundamentalism, Calvinism, orthodoxy, liberalism, neo-orthodoxy with its various manifestations, and ground of being . . . and survived. I have experienced with a sense of genuine loss the death of God. The dilemma is whether or not I ought to continue to consider myself in the Christian camp (a point you underscored in *Christianity and Crisis*, December 13, 1965). I choose to do so because I cannot disengage myself from the pervasive influence of the Man who was and is—Who? *Genitum non factum, consubstantialem patri* . . . or the Man for others . . . or a Place To Be?

The death of God . . . is there a possibility of his resurrection (sound Christian doctrine), reanimation, revivification, rebirth? Do I detect a faint stirring of hope in you that this may come about? I quote from "Thursday's Child": "thus, he has had to come out into the open about his faithlessness even though he may suspect and hope that beneath it is a passion and a genuine waiting for something that may one day get transformed into a kind of faith even better than what he has willed to lose." Do I construe correctly from this that you are also awaiting *deus redivivus?* That is my position. . . . So you see, I am an incurable optimist after all.

Forgive me my garrulity (it's one of my minor vices). As I've mentioned before, there is no community of kindred minds, radical-wise, hereabouts. . . . The religious climate is not hospitable to independent thinking. . . . It's a stifling atmosphere of conventional, old-line Christian posture, and the new theology is anathematized. How long it will be before I am excommunicated I do not know. Reluctantly I am currently displaying the mask of conformity. I fervently wish I had the audacity to tear it off and throw it away for keeps.

I feel that I have traveled a long way, but I also realize that I have not yet fully come of age, in the Bonhoefferian sense. I imagine that I am more like Thursday's Stepchild . . . and I still have far to go. Perhaps it will be a long night's journey into day.

A similar voice from a Midwestern church:

I received my copy of the October 6 issue of *The Christian Century* today and avidly read your exciting, disturbing, provocative and stimulating article. Instead of responding to the magazine (I may do this also), please permit me to take a bit of your time to bend your ear.

First, let me say that this is the best piece of theological reading that I have done lately; you really addressed me. I was able to share your feelings, if not your specific experiences. Second, what about this "small group of teachers and scholars, pastors and student workers"? You say that they are in touch with one another; how can I get in touch with this group? When and where is this major meeting taking place? Is the new journal a real possibility? I am really interested. Can you let me know?

The three motifs which you outline briefly (much too briefly) have become a part of my thinking also; however, hardly as sophisticated. I seek greater sophistication: where can I get it? Can you suggest a bibliography?

A question which plagues me and which I feel is relevant at this point is how does the institutional church, which supports your school, put up with you? You are obviously, according to all traditional standards, subverting the youth. At this point you are more honest than I am; my presbytery does not suspect me. Perhaps, it would not care; but many, if not all, of my parishioners would.

Another question: not to judge your ethics, nevertheless, how do you justify your official connection with a theological institution, especially a denominational one at that? I have thought very seriously about demitting the ministry on purely ethical grounds; I have violated my ordination vows, unless they are reinterpreted and construed to include me. And on a very practical level, as one of my closer friends accused me and rightly so, I perpetuate a lie every Sunday morning and thereby destroy myself and my hearers.

Harvey Cox in his *The Secular City* suggests leaving the ministry; I have a vested economic interest in the church. My family must eat. And further, as a friend recently told me, industry will hardly consider a former preacher, for he must be a nut or something. The response is obvious.

I have wrestled long and hard, and continue to do so, with these extremely disturbing issues. They are a serious matter with me, as they are with you. Can you provide some help? Or am I too lost on the sea of despair? My problem is not the radical nature of this kind of theologizing; my problem is where do I fit in the scheme of things. I simply do not. Is Unitarianism the only answer? Or is that even an answer?

You know the screwball thing about me is that I really enjoy working exegetically in the Biblical texts. You can imagine what my sermons are like: pure, un-adulterated crap. How can they be otherwise? I have tried and continue to weave them around a human christology, but they are like balloons filled with water.

Well, I have foisted on you some personal problems, but real problems of a parish pastor who just does not fit. And yet I must fit. Dilemma? Not really, where's the nearest headshrinker?

If you could find a niche of time to respond, I would be extremely honored to receive your reply. I would greatly appreciate any information on other "misfits" in the ecclesiastical machine, so that we might have some fellowship, in a real sense—something in com-mon.

The remaining letters, mainly from the professional community, probed deeper into the meaning and impli-cations of Hamilton's theological ideas. Take, for ex-ample, the following letter from one who heard Hamilton speak at Union Theological Seminary in the fall of 1965, and wrote to him, sharing some of her perceptive com-ments—"all in the spirit of 'holding up the prophet's hands'":

You said something like, "God was, but now is not." Here's what I mean by that: "God was" insofar as people conceived of a divine spirit up there, out there, what-have-you (Tillich: under here) and insofar as that concept had an effect upon people and upon the world. God was, in a way, "real" because people imposed their idea upon the real world and lived a certain way because of it. God "died" because men developed a better method of thinking which exposed old religious ideas to a criticism which has finally destroyed ancient imagination. But nothing really has changed in the structure and ways of the universe; it is only men's ideas that have changed. The "death of God" is in some ways most meaningful if people can understand that all we're ever talking about is ideas coming from men (where they have always come from) and not objective reality suddenly disappearing.

One student asked a most perceptive question: "If you were in the parish ministry, even in some other capacity than preaching and worship, wouldn't you undermine the one who did the preaching and led the worship?" This is another way of asking whether the new position isn't actually presented as just another absolute that cannot tolerate difference. Here I have made up a term: a "transient absolute," and I think of a parallel that is useful to me. If a doctor, even a young, inept, not too experienced doctor, takes his ways into a hospital where the practices of healing center about bleeding and the four humors, it is quite true that he will undermine what is going on there. But he is right. There is an objective certainty about the methods he uses compared to older "knowledge" which methods will, in time, triumph. So it is, in a sense, absolute! It is, however, a transient absolute— someday we may learn better thought-methods, etc., which outdate what the young doctor is now doing. But in our time and place, according to the best knowledge we have from all the fronts of learning, he is *right*. Within the ranks of modern medicine there is all kinds of room for difference of approach, opinion, etc., so no single doctor and his theory can claim absolutism; but as over against past myth and superstition, any of the variations of modern medicine are right. Ogden puts this pretty well in the September *Christian Century:* "The scientific world-picture is now a given of our situation, and any serious claim to truth must reckon with this fact. Similarly, the philosophical criticism of traditional theism, which has become increasingly extensive since Spinoza, has achieved results that are too well substantiated to be any longer ignored or explained away."

I very much like the way you answer, "Why Jesus?" I agree. But the question, as I said in the other letter I wrote to you, is not big enough; it should be, "Why *only* Jesus?" And while I'm at it, "Why *only* the Bible?" I am not satisfied to hear that these are our touchstones and chosen boundaries. Must we limit ourselves to these, and if so why? I love their insights, respond to their challenges, never wish to cut myself off from either Jesus as a model or the Bible as a source of wisdom, but I refuse their bond of limitation. I have to start with this life, with me, with the people around me, asking: "What are the real essentials? What can't we do without if we are to be better human beings? What ought we to increase and develop and celebrate and share in a grateful community of the concerned?" And I keep coming out with love, yes—so far, so good and ever so Christian—but also knowledge and beauty, which are not of Christian origin nor in the sphere of Christian concern. Yet we do, in fact, celebrate these goals; they nourish and sustain us, and without them we could hardly live as human beings. So much of our trouble in theology has been because we demeaned knowledge and steadfastly held it back; and we've been suspect of beauty as well. I personally would go sick, sick, sick on nothing but love even in its most varied manifestations. Where's all the zing of science and all the dash of art if we keep ourselves to Jesus and the Bible? If we are so insistently Christian, mightn't we miss the boat again with a too-narrow look at life? I'd like elbowroom—symbols that raise goose pimples on me, like microscopes and a cell in mitosis and dancing bodies that praise dancing, not Christian love.

I'm not convinced that wonder is out of style. True, there is a dearth of it in the "average man" or in your children and mine, but I see it as one of our very large tasks to bring alive again that sense of wonder. I don't wonder about the Almighty Hand that fashioned these stars, this cell so much—but I am in utter awe and splendid wonder at these stars, this cell. If the Cause behind the fact is gone, the fact is not a bit less wonderful. Only religion (in a wider and deeper sense than the term has ever meant) can restore genuine emotions of thanks and praise and participation in the natural universe, making people sense the wonder that lies just beside the terror at the depths of life, depending on how you look at it.

How you look at it—isn't that the whole thing? As people begin to center down to this world, leaving the projections of their own imaginations behind them, they've got to find new ways to look at the physical world with appreciation and find their own role within it instead of beyond it. And this, as I see it, is the job of religion if it can strip itself of magic. I am, I guess, most of the hated evils rolled into one: atheist, relativist, humanist, naturalist, materialist (in the Spinozan sense), but I'm not sure I'm a secularist. I am not for thinking of the church only in terms of secular involvement, although I am certainly *for* that; but when we start accumulating content that makes sense, when we find symbols that make that content powerful emotionally, when we once again take the chaos and/or meaninglessness of existence and help people look at it in a certain way, as when you hold an old piece of cheap glass in a certain way and it shines like a diamond—but only if you hold it in that certain way—when we can begin doing this for the world (and I believe with all my heart it can be done) then we won't always have to go where the people are, because the people will want to be where we are too.

One comment on the N. Y. *Times* article a few weeks ago—it was excellent and has provoked much interest. But our fatal flaw showed up at the end: here were the N. T. scholars now busily at work, taking the insights of the new theology and reworking the old text to make things come out even; and in due time they will claim, "This is the insight of the Bible." It is not! It is insight straight out of the life we live together and if we can find things here and there in the Bible that reinforce the views we cannot help holding, all well and good; let us use them and learn from them and rejoice; but we can be as free to go elsewhere. Contemporary experience is our only norm. We waste ourselves and our time reshaping the old norms to say what we're already saying without them, and all the world sees our dishonesty.

An English teacher "in an obscure Midwestern college" wrote of some "perplexities":

As nearly as I can understand it, you "death of God" theologians are not using the word "death" in the same sense most of us use it; that is, you do not conceive of a final end of God but only the kind of death which the Gospels tell us Jesus had, followed by a resurrection. It is only in such a concept as this that I can understand your speaking of "waiting for God." If you mean "death," you mean it only in such a sense as this; if the word is given any other meaning, you do not mean "death" so much as "withdrawal" or "departure." While this meaning of the "death of God" is unorthodox enough, certainly using the phrase the "death of God" makes it seem much more unorthodox than would be suggested by "the departure of God." Now, it occurs to me that the phrase you have chosen is waving a red flag in the face of orthodox Christians and will stir up opposition; indeed, you have been preached against (not by name) in the local Methodist church.

Until I thought of that, the position you ascribed to Professor Altizer did not seem to make any sense at all. By embracing the death of God, Professor Altizer hopes to bring about his rebirth. But this is pure irrational magic, on the level of planting potatoes in the dark of the moon to bring about a good crop. Then, as I say, it occurred to me that it is conceivable that you will get much opposition from orthodox groups, which are certainly in a moribund state; and that you may be hoping that the opposition to you will develop into a strong enough movement to bring God back. Thus you and Professor Altizer will have become martyrs in a good cause; the attacks on you will really be blows struck for the end you are trying to achieve. As Jesus died to bring man to God, you will have died to bring God back to man.

Am I making all this up? . . .

My personal reaction to all this is that if God is dead, even in the sense in which I understand you to use that expression, then heaven and hell are dead too and the whole system of traditional rewards and punishments with which orthodox Christianity used to deal. Modern man is left without a *why* for moral behavior. It would seem to me that one very useful task to which death of God theologians might address themselves is providing a theological *why* on which the code of Christian ethics which they continue to espouse might be substantially based. Are we to be Christs to each other because of the utilitarian "greatest good of the greatest number"? Or because the "moral sense" declares this to be self-evidently good? Or because of the satisfactions and gratifications which are to be found therein? Or why?

I hope you will forgive me for intruding on your time and especially for the tone of my last paragraph. I am an English teacher, and it is natural for me to set assignments.

A well-known Jewish spokesman for radical theology discussed the movement from his personal perspective:

Now that the publicity has settled down about the "death of God" theology, I thought I would drop you a note. I am genuinely pleased that you and the others have received the notice you have. It makes my job a great deal easier. When people suggest that I am very radical theologically, it is a comfort to be able to point to you, Tom Altizer, and the others. One might say that you have taken the heat off me to an extent. I do not know whether you have ever seen a copy of an article which I wrote about ten years ago entitled "The Symbols of Judaism and Religious Existentialism." It expresses more of the themes which are now a part of the contemporary discussion.

Recently I participated in the Conference on America and the Future of Theology at Emory University. It gave me an opportunity to meet Tom Altizer and to respond to his presentation. Briefly, I find that I share his analysis of the "death of God" as a cultural fact, but I cannot accept his apocalyptic enthusiasm over the event. This leads me in the direction of a pagan pessimism, not unlike that of Albert Camus, and a mystical nihilism. I do hope that we keep in touch and I am most anxious to meet you personally. I feel that we represent a style and a mode in theology which will be of great significance in the next twenty or thirty years. This may sound like an arrogant self-evaluation, but I think what has happened is that a new generation of theologians are taking over where Tillich has left off.

A professor of sociology and anthropology addressed the problem of whether Hamilton in all honesty should not change intellectual communities now that he has forsaken Christian theological assumptions:

I have always thought of you as an unusually bright man with a great deal of intellectual ability. The funny thing is, as an outsider I perhaps hold a conservative view on the intellectual assumptions of the theologian, for I believe that one cannot justify the existence of theology and the practice of theology, at least finan-cially supported by the churches, without the assump-tion of the metaphysical reality of God and perhaps an analysis of the traditional assumptions of Chris-tianity. In other words, I think one is playing a game and actually is dishonest by expecting the churches to support a philosophical view which is untenable from a point of view of the actual activities of the church. In other words, if the role of the minister is to teach the ethics of Christ only and to be a Boy Scout leader in the community, working for good cheer and good public relations, why not put this into the hands of other institutions which can do it more successfully than the church?

I deeply appreciate your statement in *The New Yorker*. It seems to me to be honest, but for the life of me I cannot understand how you can justify teaching theology in a seminary, or would even want to, on the basis of the theological position you seem to have arrived at, at least, for the moment. That's why I say, "Come on over and join us." Some of us who were struggling with this question ten years ago in seminary were trying to get an answer to the problems you're raising at the moment. We never got it at Colgate Rochester and we may never find it outside of the church, but at least we keep our own integrity in the bargain.

After stating his sympathies, a Baptist minister wrote, "Now, for some serious questions":

You talk of the experience of the absence of God, rather than the absence of the experience of God, which is a nice little formula but damned bothersome. First, I suspect you are talking about the absence of the experience of the Barthian God who wounds and stalks, stalks and wounds with his pursuing shadowy presence. It seems to me that if one could dare read your spiritual biography, you have found that Barthian God simply was irrelevant to anything we actually experience (whatever to hell that may mean). In other words, I am accusing you of having swallowed the Barthian giant and you are now regurgitating him. Condescending, but nicely sincere. Then, following the biographical bit, your Barthian "wholly other" meant the Bonhoefferish weak God that is wholly other from our experience, in that he is the man for others, encapsulated into Christ, allowing himself to be edged out of our grown-up world, yet like Shakespeare's flower, able to crack the rock of our sophistication. Then, along comes Pelz quoting me quoting Blake, Thou art a man, God is no more, learn thy own humanity to adore it, and everything falls into place.

We have the weak Christ here in our midsts, and that is God in that his cross, i.e., being at the disposal of others, is the ethical thrust occasionally observed in the world, and which makes unnecessary any metaphysical beyond, whether it can be adequately described for the analytical philosophers or not, and consequently we are freed to live in this world as did Christ. The only thing is, this observation is an experience known by its absence also. It is at this point of the change from Barthianism to Bonhoeffer to Hamilton that I have been making the mental charges against you of "faddism," of trying to be with it as far as the experiences of the world (modern, sophisticated, technical, *et al.*) goes. I am willing to confess that the categorizing of you in any of these brackets has been the check on the outright charge. I have no idea of how badly I may have mangled your actual intent.

Second, and more to my point, I think you and Altizer are saying too much in your very different ways. I preferred the corny "waiting for God" to the outright faith statement that God is dead. Your claim is gigantic as was the Barthian God. It smacks of the Nietzschean madman in his egomania. I suppose the negative side of a statement of where we are must be said, but it seems to me that you can't know all that you are claiming to know, in spite of all the evidence that apparently confirms your judgment. Why can't you continue to use the parable of man-woman love as a source of understanding where we are? It works, with all its demonic ramifications. Simply because a lover who controls a business allows his business to run amok does not state that he is dead, though it raises hellish questions about his maturity and responsibility. But it does raise questions, or ought to, in the beloved's mind.

Rather than that, I of course prefer this: We are the prodigal in the far country. We are living off the resources that have been given, so long ago, and so many experiences ago, that we can't quite recall how. We are able to get along quite nicely without any reminders from home. We are making it as the prodigal. Now, occasionally we hear rumors that our father is dead; sometimes we may even be greeted by one who claims to have talked to him, but for the time being—for our time—we are living without contact with him, nor with any knowledge, concern, or interest in making the contact: He may be dead, but as a matter of fact, that is something we cannot get confirmed or denied. Basically, I suppose this is an agnostic-deist sort of thing, but it is an attempt not to say too much in the face of the reality of our world. The experience that we have shared is not so much the absence of God as it is the presence of the world and of ourselves. It is this positive side that must be stated, as perhaps Harvey Cox is stating it (which I wonder about, too). We are in the world whether we want to be or not, and we are not traveling family style, we are alone. Living the style that you hint at in your book, whether by design or accident, it's hard to say. As I read this over in its badly put way, I can see that I have been lacking in manners as ever. But, at least it's something that can be got at.

A thoughtful reader who was concerned about "the conceptual adequacy" of Hamilton's position wrote:

I have serious questions concerning the conceptual adequacy of your position, and I think that ultimately some such philosophical-theological grounding is necessary for it of the nature which Tom has projected. (In that judgment, I show myself still not entirely disenchanted with some of our more recent attempts such as Bultmann and Buri [as well as the nineteenth-century liberal tradition] to redefine the Christian truth for modern ears. And with that, I am unwilling entirely to throw over the theological and philosophical resources which have been used in that attempt.) Despite these reservations, however, I could not be more sympathetic with the impulses which have driven you to make this new turn, nor with the motives you are trying to bring to expression in it. I think I indicated this fundamental sympathy in my conversations with you. Because of it, you will find in me a partner in your future attempts to find a way to say the important insight which you mean.

My one suggestion, apart from my feeling that you need to draw on philosophical and theological resources, is that, it seems to me, you must be careful to introduce a greater degree of dialectic into your position. By this I mean nothing but what your more conservative critics at the seminar voiced in a fear that you have lost the transcendent dimension. Perhaps you will finally refuse to reify that transcendent in the traditional language of God; but that is not what I mean. It simply means that while continuing to deny the "God talk," you could still find room for that dialectical principle in Protestantism which Tillich has called the Protestant principle and which some today are trying to use the principle of justification by faith to articulate (e.g., Van Harvey). A greater use of some such dialectical principle would prevent your optimism from becoming superficial and it would make room for a legitimate appreciation of much that is valuable and true in the Christian understanding of man's sinfulness. It seems to me that this could be done without at all qualifying your rejection of the "God talk" or your optimism.

Be that as it may, I mainly want to express my appreciation for the motives in your position. It is exciting to me at last to find some serious Christian thinkers who have been "smoked out" and are willing to make some radical breaks and attempts at redefining the truth to which we all, in our different ways, are attempting to give expression. I will look forward to continuing the conversation in the future.

Edited by John J. Carey

LETTERS TO THOMAS ALTIZER

Lᴇᴛᴛᴇʀs to Professor Altizer have come from laymen and clergymen, from the uneducated and from prominent professors and theologians, from all parts of the country. We have selected some representative letters to show both the indignant reaction and appreciative support of Altizer's work, as well as including some letters which raise some critical (and penetrating) questions about Altizer's contributions to the "radical theology."

First, some sharp reactions from people of different religious backgrounds:

A Wyoming sectarian, who addressed his letter to "False Prophet Alitzer" (*sic*), wrote:

I note from the newspaper your "Heresy." It's too bad people around you are shaken. There's no reason for them to be.

I address you as "False Prophet," not to be smutty or as a jesture of sarcasm, but as what you are! The only thing that bothers me any, is why you wish to blaspheme the Holy Christ and connect yourself in any way with Christianity. Your doctrine is not new, the apostles dealt with "False Prophets" the same as you— they taught the same as you. You need not call your doctrines "A New Reality." Your doctrine is no new doctrine, your digrees have failed, evidently, to acquaint [you] with the past "False Prophets" and "Doctrines of devils." The nonsencical part about you is, you contridicting yourself, saying "God is dead" and yet you wish to associate yourself with a "Dead God," and a "Dead Christianity." You're about the most nonsencical "prophet" old satan has sent out! Now, here's a few words, when you are cast into that "Lake of fire" by this "Dead Christ" you Blaspheme, what can you possibly think! You'll be worse than "speechless" as the one without the "Wedding Garment"! [The spellings of the original have been retained.]

A Wisconsin housewife, sensing that Altizer must be a part of a Communist conspiracy, wrote:

I have read of you that you believe "God is dead" but in some way you want to retain Christ.
2 Cor. 5:19—"God was in Christ reconciling the world unto Himself." God and Christ are alive in the hearts of men—so your statement is a *lie*.
You are insane—you think you are God—you are one of Satan's people—you are Antichrist.
Your man-made religion—the worship of man cult —is pagan and offensive to God and true Christians.
You cannot understand God and Scriptures, so you deny him and hate him.
You should read the Holy Bible earnestly and ask God for understanding. But that isn't what you want, is it? You are afraid of the truth. You are a Communist working in the international conspiracy against Jesus and Christians.
2 Cor. 6:14—"Be ye not unequally yoked together with unbelievers."
2 Cor. 6:17—"Wherefore come out from among them

and be ye separate, saith the Lord, and touch not the *unclean thing.*"
True Christians believe this.
John 5:39—"Search the Scripture"
2 Tim. 4:2—"Preach the Word"
Gal. 6:7—"Be not deceived. God is not mocked; for whatsoever a man soweth, that shall he reap also."

A Georgian who left The Methodist Church said:

> Your immature ravings in the press were read by me and were the reason for my finally withdrawing my membership from The Methodist Church....
> Have you *really* ever read the Bible? Don't you know that God himself will separate the ones who lived up to his commandments, accepted Christ as their Savior, etc., from those who did not profess to know God?
> You, needless to say, are on very dangerous ground. You might have got a kick out of a little notoriety in the press and having some idiotic followers listen to you as if you are the fount of all knowledge. However, all that time when measured against the time that you and I and others will either spend *with God* or *without God* is of course insignificant. We measure time because we are finite. God does not measure time, because he is infinite.
> This is a free country. You are entitled to your little say. Hell is free also.

An official in a midwestern conservative church wrote:

> Godly people everywhere are deeply grieved at your recently published so-called views on God and religion. It is inconceivable that a member of a faculty in a denominational university should have the audacity to make a statement that God is dead, and then be free

to pass these views on to young people entrusted to his care and to tamper with their faith. Psalm 53:1 perfectly describes men of your kind: "The fool hath said in his heart, There is no God. Corrupt are they, and have done abominable iniquity: there is none that doeth good." One is reluctant to apply this passage to you—you with your intelligence and training, but it is the Word of God that makes the statement. God and his Word are the anvil upon which many a scoffing and unbelieving hammer has been worn out—and they still stand unscathed.

I feel led to write you this letter to tell you that in the first five minutes after death your theology will be all straightened out. You will then face the God whom you have ignored and scoffed at. The tragedy of it all is that you will have an entire eternity to endure the remorse and regret for your folly of a misguided life, and for the harm you did to other people in leading them astray.

It is not too late to turn from your present course and to call upon God in his mercy to forgive. You are in a wonderful position to help young people in their spiritual lives if you would; but your theology can only make havoc of their faith, and God will hold you responsible.

A Phi Beta Kappa Episcopal priest protested:

As a parish priest with at least some claim to education (I have earned various degrees from Chicago, Toronto, and Oxford, am a member of Phi Beta Kappa, and was informally offered a position on the faculty of Oxford), may I say that such ideas, at least when taken out of the Senior Common Room and presented to the public by the mass media, are at least bewildering and disappointing to ordinary church people who find great meaning in the New Testament and in the Creeds. I am certainly no fundamentalist, though I admit to a certain traditionalism: partly because my vocation is to present the gospel to "ordinary" men and women, who, *pace* Bultmann and others, still find meaning in the "traditional" (i.e., post-Darwinian, post-Tübingen) Biblical imagery. Surely the problems that face the church today in communicating its message effectively are hardly due to the fact that people have become philosophers (though they may, misguidedly, have become *philosophes*); the problem is, by and large, that they have fallen victims to scientism, and the pervading humanistic agnosticism and thirst for novelty that provide the underpinnings of the Liberal Society. The problem is one of *faith*, which is a spiritual rather than an intellectual quantity. Many people no longer care to commit themselves to an Absolute; the content of selfishness has in our age taken on a cosmic, ethico-religious quality, as evidenced in the vogue of existentialism and (on a more popular level) Norman Vincent Peale-ism.

It does seem to me that this vast emergence of existential selfishness . . . is very closely related to the Biblical symbolism of the "Antichrist"; it is, perhaps, one manifestation of the Sin against the Holy Spirit: the denial of God's transcendence over a fallen creation. I'm afraid that the various manifestations of the "New Theology" and, especially, the "New Morality," will only reinforce in the minds of the unheroic godless their tendencies toward irreligion.

On the other end of the spectrum, a number of persons expressed appreciation for Altizer's insight and courage. An Episcopal priest wrote:

I am moved by your note and want to thank you. There is a remarkable acceptance at [this parish] by a lot of people who know that which they were forced to profess allegiance to is no longer even a "heteronomous" option. The phrase "God is dead" has been one of relief to many. They knew this but no one would lead the way—

Now the specifics of reconstruction are vague to them, but many are willing to participate in the birth pangs.

There are, of course, lots of mossbacks and superstitions left but then their style of life gives lie to their profession.

P.S. I will try your articles, but you are often over my head—I'm a simple parish priest.

A perplexed Wisconsin Lutheran asked Altizer for help and direction:

I am presently a member of . . . a small, almost fundamentalist, segment of the Lutheran church. My father was a life-long pastor in this group, and it was in this religious atmosphere that I was raised. I intended to become a pastor, graduated from our synod's pre-ministerial college (majoring in the classics), but could not bring myself to attend the seminary. Since I was musically inclined, I pursued music as a vocation. . . . This is my sixth year of synodical teaching on the high school and college level. I can no longer continue in this capacity if I am to remain honest with myself and with the church.

Some ten years ago I first began to think for myself and to call into question some small points of church doctrine and practice. Since that time a gradual process of liberalization and secularization has taken place. . . . Today I am almost without the organized church; yet I do not wish to let Christ go. I soak up Bishop Robinson and any other liberal writer I can lay my hands on— not because I wish to hop on the latest bandwagon but because you people are saying things which I find myself wanting to say. But to think this way and to teach in the Wisconsin Synod are irreconcilable.

The solution would seem to be obvious. Get out of the synod and teach elsewhere! However, my sense of vocation has departed along with my allegiance to the organized church. I am supposed to be a church musician and teach church music. I direct sacred choral concerts and my performing instrument is the pipe organ. When my traditional theology collapsed, so did the need for my vocation! To continue to pursue this vocation as though nothing had happened has been impossible and has brought me to the end of my rope. I wish to deal with ideas, to ask questions, to challenge people's thinking, to use the arts in this process. In short, I wish to be a part of the radical reformation that is going on within the church today, but I don't know how to go about it! I wish to talk, work, and study with others who think in this way, but I don't know who they are!

My question is: What can I do? . . . How to become part of the reformation, to most effectively help my fellowman, to follow the call which I feel to speak out? Can you help me?

A woman director of Christian education with responsibilities on a national board spoke of the need of young people:

I must admit that my first impression about your written work—based entirely on press reports—dismissed you as an academician playing around with a dangerous slogan, a language analyst who had lowered himself to popularize his view. The article "Word and History" refutes that hasty impression. For you take seriously incarnation and eschatology and then clearly indicate to me that a man no longer must talk "sacred" language to know what these words mean.

My job involves responsibility for Christian education of senior high age youth. In teaching them, I have often found that "sacredness" of the Bible, of Jesus Christ, of God a real obstacle of faith. Indeed, that "sacredness" often suggests to them a heretical meaning of faith as assent to doctrines coming to us from the past. I've often had to trick them into *reading* the Bible, but when they begin reading it as though it were a novel or another "normal" book, it sometimes becomes suddenly instructive.

I am intrigued that some of the most significant "theological" dialogue high school young people engage in in my community is stimulated today by (a) a few public high school teachers (often literature or social science teachers), and (b) bull sessions about the *actions* of persons, including nations and churches. When they self-consciously discuss theology, they often don't make good sense. When they discuss the meaning of what persons in literature and life *do*, they're more in their element and make better sense.

I am convinced that the vitality of the church in the world coming up demands the kind of dialogue you have helped initiate. Of course, sacred images die hard, and like the "demons" of the New Testament, often wreak havoc in the process of exorcism. Nevertheless, I hope you will write that next book.

A prominent theologian wrote:

I remember well our conversation at Princeton. I am utterly certain that we are going through a period of radical transition in Christian theology. I believe the period of classical Western metaphysics is over, but, as you know, I believe that we have never been suffi-

ciently concerned about the creative possibilities of the
New Testament categories of Spirit, Love, and Personal Purpose. I believe that we have seen the categories so long and so overwhelmingly in terms of our
predominate metaphysics that we find it difficult even
to understand the difference. I have never been more
amazed than to discover how open and eager non-
Christian thinkers were when they found a presentation of Spirit, Love, and Personal Purpose divorced
from the classical Western metaphysics and still having
some distinctive content to offer. I have high hopes that
competent thinkers like yourself will enter a thoroughly
creative period when you will begin to build once
again toward the new world that has to be if we are
not only to survive but go on to a creative civilization.
It is for this reason that I read your suggestive writings
with such burning interest.

Perhaps the most interesting correspondence, however,
came from laymen, clergymen, and theologians who
pressed Altizer for clarification of some of his themes and
who raised criticisms of his work.

A Jewish friend of Altizer asked about the personal
implications of Altizer's thought:

This is no time to enter into a discussion of the substance of your "new" theology, of which I have wit-
nessed the preliminary sketches. However, I'd like to
put a few questions on its newness, if any, and on its
personal meaning for you. There is first the perhaps
trivial historical fact that nontheistic Protestant theologies are no new thing to anyone from the University
of Chicago. Secondly, the "death of God" stance is no
new thing to me, and takes me back to where I was
twenty and even thirty years ago. Nietzsche is an old
friend of mine, dating back to my teens and early

twenties (and so is Blake). When I first came to the U. of C., I planned to do a creative work on Nietzsche's ethics. Nevertheless, it may well be that we may have to keep walking down that path and kicking aside the fragments of the smashed and rotting idols. (Leaving aside, of course, the myriad materialists, etc., for whom this is no problem and your crisis is no crisis—they can talk with experienced authority on a no-God secular world, which is the source of value and vitality for them.)

More important is the question of the personal meaning of the new theology for you—your life and your action. I remember once your shocked response when I told you of the nontheistic Methodist minister I knew who used kneeling-down prayer sessions to cure a parishioner of despair. You said, aghast, it was "demonic" for an atheist to pray to a God he did not believe in, in order to get things done. I was impressed then by your moral fervor and sensitivity. What does the "dead God" theologian do now? Is he like the present-day "Honest to God" Christians, described by Alasdair MacIntyre as believing "that there is no God and that it is wise to pray to him from time to time"? Or, to put it another way, why, then, stay in the church? Why remain a Christian?

I hope you don't regard this as a mean, carping, merely *ad hominem* question. All things are *ad hominem* in the Kierkegaard sense here—one should put one's money where one's mouth is. That is one of the reasons why I often find it hard to take present-day Protestant thinkers (or sayers) seriously—they always have it both ways and always keep the "living" in one sense or another. When God was dead for Felix Adler, he regretfully but decisively walked out of Judaism and started a new, nontheistic, secular faith—Ethical Culture. Similarly I walked out of Judaism once and simply fellow-wayfared in the secular light or dark, depending on how you see it. Buber affirmed views decisively at variance with accepted Jewish tradition and beliefs, while also affirming his Jewishness, but emphatically never as a Jewish theologian or minister.

Perhaps this is because there is something radically different between being a Jew and being a Christian, so that a Christian must always belong and act within the institutional forms, in order to speak as a Christian at all. Perhaps, then, what Bartley thought Bonhoeffer might have done was quite improbable, at least in a present-day Protestant context—when *everyone* belongs. Yet it would still be possible to say, "I stand aside, I will not serve, I can do no other," or some such thing. It has been done before by Christians, hasn't it? Then, indeed, the ex-Christian lambs would be out in the real secular world, in actuality and not in literary-theological imagination. . . .

A university professor from the Northeast protested:

"God is dead" substitutes one set of metaphors for another: "depth" for "height," "ground" for "Father," etc., and it may be well to do so, but metaphors are still metaphors and when, as in theology, they are used in an attempt to express the noumenal in terms of the phenomenal, they are, or can be, meaningful only because of the existential relation between subject and object. It follows, for me, from that relation (i.e., that they are correlative) that to say "God is the ground of our being" is also to say he is the ground of the world's being, and further that this is as true today as it ever was in the past. It is true of God as the divine Will or (in traditional language) God the Father, who did not "die" in Christ, since, if he had done so, the world must have ceased to exist.

On the other hand I certainly do accept an evolutionary change in the relation between man and God. But that has been possible precisely because the relation is not a simple one, but is a threefold one answering to the threefold nature of the Godhead.

Essentially, I accuse "God is dead" of the fallacy with which they charge their opponents (it is no doubt true of a few of them, particularly the fundamentalists, but they seem to insist that it applies to all of them): i.e., of conceiving of the noumenal as though it were phenomenal—and this is what I call idolatry. Their "dialectic" is based on treating the ground of existence as one among other existents, subject to the laws governing existents and in space and time, like them. God must be either here or there, either inside or outside, either up or down—like my luggage when I went on a journey, which I must either have left behind or brought with me. The technique is to impale orthodoxy, or indeed everybody else, on the horns of this ridiculously unreal dilemma and then proclaim that they have chosen the wrong horn!

For the same reason "God is dead"s' diagnosis of the bearing of science on religion strikes me as crude in the extreme and must, I believe, strike any educated physicist in the same way. I ask you, in my turn: Do you really believe, with Bishop Robinson, that space exploration has proved there is no "room" for God in the universe?

A philosopher who had had a previous opportunity to meet and respond to Altizer wrote:

I have been meaning to write to you about your fascinating article "William Blake and the Role of Myth in the Radical Christian Vision." I think that absorbing this article has done more than anything else—except meeting you—to help me understand what it is that you are really driving at. I find it very interesting that [the] question to you during the Symposium on whether your negations are "absolute" or "dialectical" [was] anticipated and explicitly answered in this article (page 463). This is a very important point, and I think that perhaps you should make more of it in your writing and speaking.

Speaking at a [place] very far removed from the papal throne, it seems to me that if Christianity admits the notion of "heresy" and "orthodoxy" at all, your views as I now begin to understand them are clearly heretical doctrine. But I am just as unimpressed by this fact (if it is a fact) as you are, since I agree with you that the notion of heresy and church control over doctrine is *itself* unchristian. This, it seems to me, is a most liberating point, and needs to be made much more of, also, in your writing and speaking. If you are interested in seeing how a philosopher approaches this same question, and comes to the same view that you do, you might read the last chapter in *Exploring the Logic of Faith* (Association Press, 1962). . . . Do you know that book? If not, I'll bet you would be interested in reading it.

Another thing about your "William Blake and the Role . . ." article that interested me very much was your radical agape doctrine. Are you aware of the many links that tie you to the (almost) equally radical agape views of Nels F. S. Ferré? This is especially noteworthy when you link it with his sharp rejection of "being" as adequate for an understanding of God's essential nature. He takes both "being" and "becoming" as being inferior (philosophically and theologically) to agape as interpreting the Christian understanding of God. Have you yet worked your way through *The Christian Understanding of God?* If not, I wager you would find it fascinating reading. . . .

You remark in your article that secular minds are likely to see your position as atheistic. I think not. Mine is a pretty secular mind, and I see your position as religious to the core. You have simply altered the image of God by taking the kenotic perspective with ultimate seriousness. I see this as very far from an abandonment of theism in general, though of course it is a far cry from traditional theistic positions. My problem, as a secular philosopher, is rather one of attempting to evaluate the truth, or lack thereof, which may be claimed by your imagery.

Are you attempting to say something that is more than a report on the individual consciousness of a few men? That is, are you making claims that are supposed to be publicly reliable, i.e., of more than autobiographical interest? If so, what are the implications of your "new mythology" for behavior? What specific expectations are we led to? If man's warlike propensities were to blow up this planet, would that count against your apocalyptic expectations? Or would it be a confirmation of them? Or neither of these? Your answers here will help me get my teeth more firmly into what your views involve.

I am still unconvinced, however, by your defense of why it is that Jesus should mean so much in the current situation. Or at least I am confused about why Jesus should mean so much to Christians but not be essential, in some way, to non-Christians. If your proclamation of radical kenosis is true, then surely "saying the name of Jesus" is not optional. How do you propose to resolve this tension?

A noted Jewish author observed:

. . . The dead God is surely being mourned and undoubtedly enjoys in his insensate finger a stirring of delight at the obsequies. I wish I could believe that

what you and the Hamilton-Vahanian axis . . . say is
more than a rhetorical transcript of a series of trau-
matic schisms in Western history, that you are (and I
don't say this disrespectfully) throwing up a big bal-
loon and letting others watch it explode while you hunt
madly for the intermediate and real truth—which may
be, may it not be, that man is dead. And the death of
man (since we are not talking biologically) is as apt a
metaphor for the dragging emptiness of human life
and passion as is the death of God. . . .

A theologian reported on the European readiness to
respond to Altizer's thought:

Although all that I have heard about you has been
from Americans, I think you may find that the situation
in European theology may be more nearly ready to
read your work with appreciation than either of us had
supposed. It seems quite clear to me that the Bultmann
school, at least, is disintegrating. The Old Marburger
meeting this year was unimpressive, but I was excited
to discover that many of the participants are highly
restive and tend to resent any repetition of Bultmannian clichés. Some of them want desperately to talk
about the "God problem" in ways that Bultmannian
orthodoxy forbids. This means an interest in both natural theology and atheism that I had not expected.
Van Buren was mentioned several times in this connection, and the last day was devoted to a lecture and
discussion about Wittgenstein. Here at Mainz, Braun,
as you know, represents his own brand of Christian
atheism and Pannenberg favors natural theology, although not usually under that name. They are by far
the two most influential members of the faculty. . . .
    In general, however, I found what little I could see
of the theological situation in England depressing.

Certainly English Methodism is completely out of touch with the wider world, and I got much the same impression of the Church of England theologians. The most interesting Methodist I met was a young fellow who had been awakened to the wider world by a year's study at Perkins. Things are changing when one must go from England to Texas to escape provincialism. I was shocked to find that Blackwell's carries virtually no books published in America and not many published on the Continent.

The Future of
the Radical Theology:
The Theologians
Speak for Themselves

PART IV

The Future of
the Radical Theology:
The Theologians
Speak for Themselves

William Hamilton

QUESTIONS AND ANSWERS
ON THE RADICAL THEOLOGY

QUESTION 1: What God is referred to in the phrase the "death of God"?

The "death of God," as the radicals use it, does not mean that some ways of thinking or talking about God in traditional Christianity are done for. It means that no ways are possible. The "God" meant in the phrase "death of God" is the God in the phrase "I believe in God the Father Almighty, Maker of heaven and earth." The God whose death is believed in is the Christian God. "Death of God" does not refer to a disappearance of a psychological capacity. Let me put it this way. Faith in God in the classical Christian tradition has always meant this: an act of passionate, personal daring and courage can be made, and when it is made, a real other is made known, over against man, making demands and making Himself known. This is the meaning of faith in God. It is this God of faith, known in this way (as against the God of religion or culture) who is no more.

QUESTION 2: Are radical theologians Christians?

Yes, because the "death of God" is now (mainly but not entirely) being talked about by Christians. Yes, be-

Previously unpublished.

cause it is the Christian God that is referred to in the phrase. Yes, because the "death of God" is an affirmation that does not disable or block, but acts as enabling things, making possible Christian allegiance not possible along other lines. But what is the proper definition of a Christian in this context? Two answers can be given. In one sense, the Christian is defined by his choice of comrades. Whom does he seek out? Whose questions and answers are his? Who makes the noises he wishes to make? "Death of God" is a Christian affirmation in this sense. The Christian is also a man in relation to Jesus, and the radical theologian affirming the "death of God" claims to be Christian in this second sense as well. (See questions 10 and 11).

QUESTION 3: Would the radical theologians call themselves agnostics, or atheists, or antitheists?

"Atheist" would be the closest. Agnostic suggests maybe, and "death of God" is not a maybe theology. Antitheism suggests an aggressiveness about others' views that the radicals don't have. But if they are atheists, they are atheists with a difference. Perhaps the difference can be put in this way. Traditional atheism believes that there is now no God and that there never has been, beliefs in God of the past being deception, ignorance, fear. Radical theology believes that there was once a time (Bible, sixteenth century, for example) when having a god was appropriate, possible, even necessary. But now is not such a time. There was once, and is not now. The present of the radical is like that of the atheist, but the memories are different. The radical can say yes to the Christian past; the atheist cannot.

QUESTION 4: Isn't radical theology just another form of humanism?

It is humanism, if humanism means a belief that there

are no viable objects of loyalty beyond man, his values, his communities, his life. But it is a Christian humanism.

QUESTION 5: Why have you insisted on the phrase "death of God"? Just because it gives offense?

It is an offensive phrase, but we have not chosen it to give offense. We have chosen it partly because we wish to relate to the tradition of religious thought in the past century that has made use of it, but primarily because it expresses exactly what we wish to express—the sense of a possession that has been taken away, a possession we do not expect to be made good, to come back. Thus, the traditional words—absence of God, or silence, or disappearance, or eclipse—all live within the world of a loss that is temporary, short-ranged, soon to be removed. And whatever we expect or hope for, the object of hope is not the Christian God.

QUESTION 6: If "death of God" is somehow an event, then presumably it is an event that may be said to have happened sometime. When?

As long as you see that "death of God" is a complex event, one that cannot be simply pointed to, then the "when" question can be accepted. There are three parts to my answer to the question:

1. The coming of Jesus as the self-emptying of God is part of the "death of God." Here is God taking on sin, suffering, and mortality. Here is the end not only of religion, and transcendent gods of power and sovereignty, but the beginning of the disappearance of the Christian God himself.

2. If the incarnation is, so to speak, the enabling part of the event of the death of God, the nineteenth century is that time when the death itself is predicted, believed in, lived out. The Christian God, in Europe and America, is dying by departing wholly from the world (deism) or

collapsing into the world (romanticism, Marx, Ibsen) between 1789 and 1914. The first date suggests the problem of the relation of regicide and deicide, and the second reminds us of D. H. Lawrence's comment that God died in 1914. One of the immediate tasks of radical theology is a thorough interpretation of the idea of the "death of God" in the nineteenth century. We need a wholly different nineteenth century than the one traditional Protestant theology bequeathed to us.

3. But there is a third part of the "when" answer, and that is now, here, mid-twentieth-century America. In a way, Nietzsche's madman (himself) was right in saying that he had come too soon. There is something about our time and place that is making the event prepared by the incarnation and analyzed by the nineteenth century come home. The twentieth century is proving to be a time when the "death of God" can be affirmed without guilt, fear, or sadness. It was Wallace Stevens who wrote: "To see the gods dispelled in mid-air and dissolve like clouds is one of the great human experiences. It is not as if they had gone over the horizon to disappear for a time; nor as if they had been overcome by other gods of greater power and profounder knowledge. It is simply that they came to nothing."

QUESTION 7: This leads to another question. If today is a special part of the historical event of the death of God, if it is being experienced by men in various ways today, would you excuse a personal question and tell me what is the special character of your experience of the "death of God"? Or would you object to the phrase "experience of the death of God"?

No, I think the phrase makes some sort of sense. The experience is for me a complex one, made up of a number of strands, each inconclusive in itself. It does not entail a discovery of a new way of knowing (van Buren's book), or a reflection on the significance of the seventeenth-century scientific revolution (Wren Lewis), or a simple statement of the irrelevance of God to modern man (Braun). There are perhaps five points that can be mentioned without expansion.

1. *The Bonhoeffer theme.* Here I would put my development of Bonhoeffer's idea of man come of age, the end of religion, the breakdown of the idea of God as problem solver and need meeter. God is not needed, even on the boundary or in the depths, to do things the world cannot do.

2. *The Dostoevsky-Camus theme.* The problem of suffering as written about by such writers, and as lived out in the twentieth century, has put an end, I think, to classical doctrines of Providence, and thus to the very center of the Biblical doctrine of God. A God to whom could be ascribed the death of the six million Jews in our time would be a monster.

3. *The theological theme.* Part of the "death of God" theology is a very conventional witness to the breakdown of the Barthian–neo-orthodox theological period in Protestantism. (Perhaps, as Michael Novak's recent *Belief and Unbelief* suggests, neo-orthodoxy is now ready to be taken up by the younger Catholics.) It is at the point of its solution to the problem of knowledge of God that its breakdown has been most tellingly felt—the doctrine of revelation. "We cannot know God," the traditional formulation of the doctrine of revelation went, and we would still agree. "But he has made himself known in Jesus Christ," they went on; and we would confess that we no longer have any means of making connections with this confession of a knowledge being given. (Incidentally, another witness to the end of the Barthian interlude is the recovery of interest in natural theology among some

of the younger theologians. A lot has been promised, but little produced, one should note.) A passage from Paul Tillich will clarify my point. "So the paradox got hold of me that he who seriously denies God, affirms him. Without it I could not have remained a theologian." (*The Protestant Era,* pp. xiv–xv.) This came with liberating force to a whole generation of American Christians, and still does, I presume. It takes the experience of denial of God and names it "faith." It seems to make not having a god, unfaith, impossible, since all the experiences that might count against God become in effect further content for the very idea of faith itself. It is just this confusion of having and not having, of saying yes with saying no, this paradox that kept the young Tillich a theologian, that has collapsed. And one might add: without rejecting this paradox, I could not have remained a theologian.

4. A fourth element might be described as an affirmation of a change in the way man stands before his world. Certain kinds of experiences of dependence, wonder, awe, are no longer available to man, and thus not available as experiences on which to base an understanding of God. (See question 18 for a more careful look at this point.)

5. Finally, the "death of God" means that there is an increased confidence in those nontheistic forms of explanation of man's experiences of moral obligation, need of judgment, longing for healing or community that the arts and the sciences provide us. The "death of God" does not imply the disappearance of the mystery, richness, complexity of life; but it does say that God can no longer be a word, a name, or a concept appropriate to explain these things. (See questions 16 and 19 for further comments along this line.)

QUESTION 8: There seems to be a certain moral arrogance in the phrase "death of God." It would appear that it not only describes

something you say has taken place in a
particular community but it also appears to
insist on that experience for everyone.

There is a problem here. I certainly don't want to
trivialize the idea of the "death of God" by claiming
merely that this thing has happened to me and perhaps
a few friends. We are not describing a psychological
shift. The "death of God" is not merely private, subjective, psychological. It points to something that has
taken place in the world of reality. This side of our claim
is the one that seems pushy and arrogant. There is one
way to neutralize that arrogance, in part. And that is to
note that the radical theologians, along with a good many
others in the Western world today, have really accepted
the relativistic spiritual and intellectual situation in which
we live. No one—no Christian, no non-Christian—has
either a handicap or a head start in the intellectual free-
for-all. No one of us, religious or nonreligious, can claim
that we contain something that makes allegiance to us
necessary, inevitable, by definition superior to all other
allegiances. None of us bears anything necessary; only
something possible. Our theology of mission consists,
therefore, not of proofs that we make better liberal demo-
crats, whole persons, facers of tragedy than anyone else,
but just the demand that we, along with others, be tested
by the quality of personal and corporate lives we elicit.
By their fruits, and not their apologetic theologies, shall
you know them and decide whether they merit your free
choice.

QUESTION 9: I take it that somehow the functions performed by God in traditional Christianity
are of interest to the radicals. What does
the god-work?

There are two answers that I see to that, answers based
on two different ways of stating the function of the

Christian doctrine of God. In one sense, the functions of
a doctrine of God are such things as: providing a test
and source for forgiveness; providing a ground for personal and social judgment, a standpoint from which
culture may be criticized; providing a means by which
comfort and hope may be offered in time of distress.
Functions like this are taken over in radical theology by
the human community. Men must do whatever forgiving
is to be done; men must comfort the bereaved, learn to
face their own deaths and the deaths of loved ones, men
must judge, rebuke, provide the critical and prophetic
perspectives on all finite structures. Men in their human
communities. If the human community as presently
formed is not able to perform these functions adequately,
then—on precisely the basis that these functions must be
performed—that should be changed so that their performance is adequate. Along these lines, what once was
done by God is done by social change, politics, even
revolution. And the corruption of men in community is
checked and balanced by other men in different communities. This procedure is hardly mysterious to an
American living under the Constitution. In another sense,
the functions of the doctrine of God can be defined
somewhat differently, as the focus of trust, the center
of loyalty, the meaning of love, something like what
Tillich calls the object of ultimate concern. (I obviously
have to eschew "ultimate" here, for it very nearly bears
the idea of God within it by definition—primary concern
would be a possible restatement of Tillich's phrase.) I
am not inclined to make the human community take
over these functions. For radical theology, though in
quite different ways (when you compare Altizer and
me, for example), Jesus performs these functions. (See
questions 10 and 11.) I have a friend who is specializing
in spotting the "latent theism" in the radical theologians,
and of course we have to be very clear at this point.
One has to answer questions like this one—what does

the work for you that God does in the classical vision?
—and one must try to do it without importing a covert
doctrine of God in the back door after pushing it out
the front.

QUESTION 10: What Jesus do you mean?

I have written elsewhere about the importance of dis-
cerning ways in which Jesus may be found in the world
—by finding him concealed in the struggle for truth,
justice, beauty, or by becoming Jesus to the neighbor in
the world. And this approach is important, but it is un-
stable unless one sees that it must be based on the New
Testament picture. The Jesus of the New Testament,
then, is the answer I would give to your question. This
raises many questions, and it implies, of course, a certain
attitude to the problem of historical method and the
credibility of the Gospel accounts. Jesus can be known,
I am claiming; enough in the record can be trusted, so
that the kind of thing he did, the way he stood before
men, the way he taught, suffered, and died, can be discerned and believed. For example, I take it that Bornkamm's *Jesus of Nazareth* can stand as a statement of a
consensus of what can be known. Sometimes we know,
and then obey; sometimes we obey in order to know.
Albert Schweitzer's picture of obedience to Jesus built
on the wreckage of Jesus' historical actuality is important
here: I'm thinking of the famous final sentence on *The
Quest of the Historical Jesus* when Schweitzer says that
"to those who obey Him, whether they be wise or simple,
He will reveal Himself in the toils, the conflicts, the sufferings which they shall pass through in His fellowship,
and, as an ineffable mystery, they shall learn in their own
experience Who He is."

QUESTION 11: I would have thought you would be more
                embarrassed than you seem to be about
                the fact that you say very nice things

about Jesus, even make a great deal of
him, while at the same time you say no
to what was one of his main emphases, the
need for absolute trust in God the Father.
Can you really maintain a loyalty to Jesus
without a loyalty to God?

This is, from my point of view, the most important
theological question that can be asked of us. Professor
Altizer solves the problem more readily than I by his
apocalyptic definition of Jesus, more Blakean than Biblical, as the one who is born out of God's death. I am not
yet ready to give up *sola scriptura*, and thus my answer
must be more complex and tentative. It is not an answer,
but an interesting and relevant fact, that a number of
New Testament scholars today are doing their research
and thinking in the context of the radical theology.
Robert Funk and Edward Hobbs are two Americans of
whom this is true, and the German scholar Herbert
Braun's work is a deliberate attempt to develop a New
Testament Christology without God: see his essay "The
Problem of New Testament Theology" in *The Bultmann
School of Biblical Interpretation: New Directions,* edited
by James M. Robinson. I think I would begin my own
answer in this way. Early in the nineteenth century we
had to face, under the early impact of historical criticism,
both facts that Jesus was firmly committed to demon
possession as the meaning of mental and physical illness,
and that we were not so committed and needn't be. But
obedience to Jesus was not destroyed. Later, at the time
of Darwinian controversy, we had to face another instance of Jesus' full participation in the thought forms of
his day—the three-story, primitive cosmology. But we do
not go to the Bible for science, we were rightly told, and
obedience to Jesus was not hurt. At the close of the century we had to face an even more disturbing fact—the

fact brought before us by Weiss and Schweitzer that Jesus was completely committed to the apocalyptic views of the Judaism of his day, and that he believed in some sense or other, in an end to the world and in a "coming" associated with that end. He proved, we said carefully, to be wrong about these matters, but not even his commitment to this eschatology proved to be an obstacle to a full Christian loyalty to him. In *Jesus and His Coming*, to be sure, the Bishop of Woolwich tries to exonerate Jesus from these eschatological views, but I do not think his brilliant argument finally convinces. Schweitzer himself showed us one way in which the eschatology, though literally wrong, guaranteed Jesus' eternal relevance to all ages; Bultmann showed us another, according to which the literal forms of the eschatological myths could be translated into tones of moral urgency and radical demand. My point is already made. If Jesus' demonology and cosmology and eschatology were taken as first-century views, appropriate then, not so now, needing reinterpretation and understanding but not literal assent, what is inherently different about Jesus' *theology?* Is there any inherent reason why Jesus' dependence on God as Father—admittedly a central idea to him (but surely no more central than his eschatological expectations)—should not prove to be one of these ideas, central to an understanding of him and his work, but not necessarily transferable to us? We would have to be able to say what has happened in our time to make that idea, so central to the first century, dispensable today, just as we can now say why the demon theory of disease is inadequate for our medical understanding. I think we can say what has happened, and that is the meaning of the event "death of God" as in part at least an event that is just now taking place in our own time. (See the third part of my answer to question 6 and the whole of the answer to question 7 for a little more detail.)

QUESTION 12: What can you make of prayer?

If prayer is defined as a religious form of address to a personalized being called God, then we can make nothing at all of it. But this is a very poor definition of prayer, and radical theology will need to state more exactly than it is now able, just what it is that lies behind acts of adoration, intercession, and praise, for example, and to what extent these can be recovered without a doctrine of God. I would further assume that in certain techniques of meditation, particularly Buddhist ones where no God is involved, some ways of dealing with personal prayer in the radical context might be found. What public worship might mean, what the celebration of the "death of God" might mean as a liturgical act, this kind of thing we are just beginning to ask ourselves. You may have seen on the CBS evening news some time ago a requiem for the death of God. I'm inclined not to think about requiems when thinking along these lines, for the death of God is not a sorrowful death really. I am more inclined to think of celebration, and of comedy.

QUESTION 13: Do you believe in life after death?

Since the basis for the classic Christian hope is not human immortality but the character of God, the radical theology is simply without a belief in life after death. It must speak of our mortality, our finiteness, without knowing or even believing anything else. This means that radical theology must speak more earnestly of the need, here and now, of facing death, befriending it, withdrawing from it the power to terrify or to make us afraid. "And life is the destiny you are bound to refuse until you have consented to die," Auden has written. Consenting to die, then, becomes a part of affirming life. From this it should be clear that the radical theology can respond deeply to the death of Jesus, but scarcely to the resurrection as abolition of death. (See the answer to question 16, especially the comment on death as a sacred event.)

QUESTION 14: Is the radical theology consciously pointing to a new kind of Christianity?

I am enough of a Calvinist to be afraid of the sectarian implications of questions like this, and I am sure there are a good many unfriendly observers of the movement waiting for our arrogance to take this form, with new liturgies, new churches, and perhaps even new saints. So my answer would be no, in most of my moods, though there are a number of radicals who are inclined to see the development in terms of Joachim of Floris' third age of the Spirit. This both interests and horrifies me.

QUESTION 15: Isn't radical theology another reductionist strategy like the old liberalism, trying to see how little Christianity can be carried, so as to appeal to modern scientific man?

Radical theology is, in terms of its content, clearly "reduced," when compared to various old and new orthodoxies. But it is not self-reduced for strategic reasons: to appeal to modern man, or to attract people influenced by science or Oxford philosophy or despair. It has no interest in contemporaneity or relevance, for their own sakes. It is not that we want to appeal to something—secularism, say—that is out there; but because something has happened to us which we are bound to accept and, accepting it we want to see what this entails for the Christian profession.

QUESTION 16: How would radical theology describe what men call experiences of wonder, reverence, awe, the sacred?

If it is true that radical theology has no wish to flatten man's experience of life out to the visible and testable, it is going to have to find some way of interpreting and affirming those elements of wonder, of awe, of reverence, even of the sacred. It just will not use the idea of God in its systems of explanation, but instead whatever in the realm of art, natural science, social science, psychology, that might be most appropriate and illuminating. This means that there might even be such a thing as a godless form of the sacred, experiences of the sacred with a validity apart from any need for a theistic explanation. What would a godless sacred look like? It would certainly involve some kind of experience of the other, the not-self, and it would also have the element of the uncontrollable. It is doubtless true that many roads to the sacred are cut off for modern men in their technological culture; perhaps the way to the sacred via holy men, holy books, holy gestures in the religious sense has become impossible for more and more of us. But may it not be that the experience of sex can become a kind of sacred event for some today? I am not referring to the kind of pseudopious nonsense found among Christians who enjoy being well thought of by Hugh Hefner, but I am referring to the astonishing idea of the sacred in the following passage from *The Scarlet Letter:*

> "We are not, Hester, [Dimmesdale is speaking] the worst sinners in the world. There is one worse than even the polluted priest! That old man's revenge has been blacker than sin. He has violated, in cold blood, the sanctity of a human heart. Thou and I, Hester, never did so!"
> "Never, never," whispered she. "What we did had a consecration of its own. We felt it so! We said so to each other! Hast thou forgotten it?"

Here is an astonishing event—the idea of a sexual relationship, outside of marriage, in the midst of Puritan New England, possessing a sacredness that does not seem to require the idea of God. Perhaps as well death can become a sacred event for some in the time of the death of God. The death of Jesus has always been sacred in a conventional sense for Christianity: pointing uniquely to the character of the divine love and will. For the radical Christian, Jesus' death is sacred in a godless sense: it bears the full meaning of Jesus' own life and work, and it shows the way man is to stand in his world. But apart from the death of Jesus, what would it mean to say that death in general can become a sacred event? What is meant of course is not our actual dying, but our preparation for dying, our living with death. Is not something like this present in the Gettysburg address when Lincoln declared that neither he nor his hearers could consecrate the ground, not because God alone could, but because "the brave men, living and dead, who struggled here, have consecrated it, far above our poor power to add or detract"? (See question 13.) However fruitful these particular approaches may be, the radical theologian, having chosen to live as a Christian without God, has a special responsibility for not ignoring the realm of life's mystery, tragedy, wonder, and holiness, and of finding structures and images, even more adequate than the traditional pictures of God, to interpret these dimensions of life.

QUESTION 17: Bishop Robinson recently spoke about God in terms of word and reality, and said that for him the word "God" is either dead or dying, virtually useless, but the reality to which the word has traditionally pointed is very much intact. I take it this is much the position of Harvey Cox as well. Would you comment on this and distinguish your position from this mere avoidance of a traditional word?

We are at the heart of the nominalist-realist controversy when we raise a question like this, and I suppose the thing to say is that we are all nominalists now. So the word-reality separation will have to stand. But without wishing to back into realism (through some theory of symbolism, myth, or view of the word as participating in the reality which it names, etc.), radical theology finds that its task is not to be simply described as the avoidance of the word "God." Such an avoidance is fairly common in the modern period; God has become "ground," "depth," "creativity," "love," "the Supremely Worthful," and still managed to do his traditional work. Such re-namings are still in the realm of the doctrine of God. For the radical theology the word "God" is gone, and the traditional reality is so substantially altered (see next question below) that no mere new name, word, or phrase will do, but only a thorough and wide-ranging attempt to think through the whole of Christian thought to see what it means to do without the Christian God—not just some of the odder formulations, but everything—from Rom., ch. 8, to last Sunday's prayer of adoration. At some points—eternal life, for example—no reformulation would appear to be possible. Doing without God means doing without eternal life (see question 13). At other points—forgiveness (see question 9, first part) and the idea of the holy (see question 16)—doing without God does not prove to be too debilitating, and some sort of reformulation can be provided. So we can say that while the word has gone, sometimes the reality behind the word has also gone, and sometimes it hasn't.

QUESTION 18: What do you mean, the traditional reality behind the word "God" has substantially altered?

This is the best way, I think, to start on that question. The "death of God" means two closely related things:

1. Certain basic experiences of awe—reverence, wonder, the tragic, the holy, the mysterious—are as real and

inevitable today as they always have been, except that radical theology claims that they neither derive from nor point to the Christian God. Secular, or nontheistic forms of interpretation must be found to illuminate them. (See question 16.)

2. Here I come to the actual question. Other human experiences, at one time among those on which belief in God had been grounded, are not so unquestioned, so universally available to men today. Man's experience of his world is the same, and it is different. Take, for example, the idea of dependence before the vastness of nature, an ancient mood with a profound religious meaning in the past. I would claim that this kind of dependence is not as inevitable today as it has been. The other night I was out in the backyard with one of my children, hunting up some constellations for his science homework. After we had finished, and had stood there a while, I thought of my youthful experience of standing beneath a clear starry sky, and how small and reverent those experiences had made me feel. Would the same be true of my son? After a few minutes he said, looking up, "Which ones did we put up there, Dad?" Here is a new man-world relation, and the basic element is not dependence but dominion (to give it another Biblical word) and control. One finds this feeling among biologists, medical researchers, and many in the space program. This is a homely but significant example of what it means to say that man's experience of the world is undergoing some profound changes, and it is changing at precisely those points that make the idea of cosmic dependence pointing to dependence on God impossible to believe. (See question 7, especially part four.)

QUESTION 19: In a recent *Look* article, President Bennett of Union gave what he called four intimations that for him require the Christian doctrine of God:

1. The fact of human loyalty and self-sacrifice and his inability to imagine that should our world be utterly destroyed someone would not be around to remember it.
2. The sense of absolute obligation.
3. The impulse to worship, and the possibility that without God, man will worship a false god or an idol.
4. The actual experience of healing, of grace in our common life.

Would you comment on these four points?

I appreciated President Bennett's article that the question refers to, not because I agreed with it, but because of the tone. He brings the debate to the point where it should be brought (as do such critics as Gilkey of Chicago and Maguire of Wesleyan as well)—what are those human realities that are claimed to require (or not to require) the doctrine of God for their full and complete understanding? So Bennett's point is the right kind of point, but I cannot, of course, agree with his specific arguments. That altruism requires the idea of God; that the idea of a cosmic catastrophe wiping all trace of life away requires the idea of a cosmic rememberer; that moral obligation, the impulse to worship, the experiences of being helped and healed, lead to what Christians have called God—all this seems to me to be excessive description of, for the most part, obvious facts. Obligation and altruism seem to permit doctrines of God for some, but I know of no way in which they can be said to be necessary. The simplest way of stating why such examples fall short for me is to cite my own experience of moral responsibility over the past years, which has entailed, from World War II since, the learning of moral sensitivity from non-Christian communities and men.

Having learned so much from so many, I cannot see myself elevating the pupil over the teacher as a matter of inevitability. These are all real human experiences that Bennett cites though his point about being unable to imagine a destroyed world without somebody around to remember us strikes me as a little frantic and peculiar. They simply resonate differently for different men today. For some they say "God." For some they do not. I cannot see how our theoretical formulations can get around this empirical fact. Is the latter group simply foolish, misguided, or wrong?

QUESTION 20: In a recent article, it is stated that if God is dead, man has no chance of being faced with ultimate, radical judgment on his life and culture. What would you say to that?

I would simply deny that on the grounds that a radical judgment on self and culture can emerge in many ways. If someone confesses that he would become a reactionary conformist without belief in the God of Amos, I'd say, then by all means believe in the God of Amos. The radical or revolutionary ethic in the radical theology comes in one sense out of loyalty to Jesus and in another sense out of the needs of the human community itself. (See questions 21, 22, 23, and question 9, first part.)

QUESTION 21: Isn't there still some moral danger in doing without the judgment of God? I'm thinking of what Berdyaev wrote in his book on Dostoevsky: "If there be no God, to love man means to deify him, to revere him as an absolute—hence the dangerous notion of the man-God which lies in wait for us to enslave and devour the individual."

Man must be faced by a standard of judgment beyond himself. He cannot be trusted to be his own judge. But the judgment that must be brought to him is the judgment he must receive in his communities—his communities of work, of play, or of worship, and the judges are his peers. I see just as much likelihood that man, having a god, will try to become one, as I see that man without a god will become a moral monster. I do not think that we can equate godlessness with arrogance any longer in the Western world.

QUESTION 22: Then you would not agree with the cry of Ivan Karamazov, that if there is no God, then everything is permitted?

No, and I don't even think Ivan believed that himself. I think evil or reactionary or corrupt behavior is as possible for men with gods as without. There is a statement of Nietzsche's that partly puts the other side of the coin: "If there were gods, then how could I stand not to be one?" This suggests that having a god leads to man confusing himself with god, and this kind of confusion is less likely in the man without a god. The fruitlessness of the suggestion that only Christians can be safe from arrogance is shown by comparing two good Presbyterians on our war in Vietnam—Kennan and Rusk. I am sure that their religious views lead directly, in both cases, to their political positions, and that Kennan is right and Rusk is terribly wrong. There is no doubt that this question is very important in many traditional Christian estimates of the radical theology. I have friends who actually find themselves believing that I am bound to become a more immoral person as a result of moving to the "death of God" position.

QUESTION 23: You mean you won't?

I may, but that won't be the reason.

QUESTION 24: This is a sociological question. How did the "death of God" controversy break into media and circles ordinarily impervious to theological ideas?

This is a very mysterious question that I really cannot answer satisfactorily. It has several parts. There is first a problem of why the controversy has moved into church circles so readily; the world of sermon, denominational magazine, Sunday school class, and so on. Atheism is as old as Christianity, yet some receptions of the phrase "death of God" suggest that today's is the first appearance of the idea on the globe. I suppose we have something by the tail here, and have served to open up some of the lines of communication between pastor and lay people that have been pretty badly clogged. Quite apart from whether the radicals themselves are honest, they may have made honesty possible in the life of the church. But if this were all, then the radical theology would be a minor ecclesiastical event, worth a short note in *Time*, perhaps, an irritated editorial in *The Christian Century*, and then forgotten. What is not at all clear is why the "death of God" controversy burst into the secular media in the fall of 1965, and pretty much stayed there throughout the academic year, not even submitting to the immediate assurances of important church people and journals that it was a fad and it, too, would pass, like the snow. It began as a public event in three separate places. A staff writer of *The New Yorker* began with Bishop Robinson and stumbled onto the American radicals almost by accident. He had been working on his article for over a year before its appearance in December, 1965. It was a very poor article, but it included extended quotations from technical theological journals and became a means of theological communication to intellectuals of all sorts who barely tolerate *The New Yorker*, but who would never darken page one of a theological article. A second source of the fall explosion was Edward Fiske, the young religion writer for *The New York Times*. Fiske, unlike many religious journalists in New York, is not dependent on seminaries and publishers and professors for his material. He gets it himself, and is a very able and gifted writer. He had read, the spring before, an article I had written in *The Christian Scholar*, and worked for some time, off and on, on his article that finally appeared in the *Times* in October, right after the newspaper strike had been settled. This soon was distributed all over the country as part of the *Times* news service, and became the basis for rather inept rewrite jobs by other newspaper and wire-service religion editors. From there on in, the newspaper articles, with some notable exceptions (*Newsday, The National Observer*, the *Chicago Daily News*), were either rewrites of Fiske's original or rewrites of rewrites of Fiske. The third source of the controversy occasioned by the publicity barrage was an article, also in October, written by the religion editor of *Time*. This was not a bad article, but it had many of the marks of the hasty *Time* products: superficial, not based on effective interviews, clever, and horrified-pious in point of view. (This last in contrast to the later cover story that *Time* did on the "death of God" controversies for their Easter [April 8] issue; again, very superficial and hasty, poorly researched, but much less irritated, hostile, more relaxed and accepting in tone. The psychological distance between these two *Time* pieces is perhaps a very instructive fact.) The occasion for the *Time* article in October was not a call to Union Seminary or a lunch with a publisher—the ways most of the *Time* religion pieces get built, apparently. The occasion appeared to be the appearance in *The Christian Century*, a deteriorating Protestant weekly earnestly monitored by *Time* and *Newsweek*, and increasingly (alas) by *The New York Times*, of a series of several articles entitled "How I Am

Making Up My Mind." Unfortunately for it, as it turned out, *The Christian Century* had asked van Buren, Altizer, and me for pieces in this series and we all got them done on time and into publication in the summer and the early fall. It seemed like a cruel blow, and *Time* decided to declare the "death of God" theology fully present and alive. The thing to note in all this is that the actual body of writing appropriately belonging to the radical or "death of God" school was very small, and except for a few asked-for pieces of journalism, it was in the form of either book or technical theological article. Newspaper, mass magazine coverage, television interview, and debate—all this followed, until the reaction overwhelmed the original event (just like in the Fourth Gospel?) and the whole thing became a pseudo event in the public world in which angry men were fighting non-existent enemies, and people were reacting to things never spoken. It is relatively simple to state why Bishop Robinson's *Honest to God* delivered the impact it did; it is less easy to answer this in terms of the two recent American versions, the enthusiasm surrounding *The Secular City*, and the not-exactly-enthusiasm surrounding the "death of God" controversy. Anything that can elicit so many foolish statements from so many good and true men cannot be all bad.

QUESTION 25: Do you consider yourself an evangelist for your position?

Yes and no. I really believe that the radical theology provides a way for one to stand and think as a Christian today, and to me it is an exciting and demanding adventure in many ways. I've had to be very careful, however, to avoid giving the wrong kind of offense to a number of people, some colleagues included, who feel that the radicals are mere fad-mongering journalists or evangelists out for converts, and not serious theologians.

QUESTION 26: Have many of your students "signed up"?

Remarkably few as a matter of fact, and somewhat to my relief, I suppose. I have fewer students who agree with my position now than I used to have when I was in my late Bonhoeffer period.

QUESTION 27: But you still travel around and talk about the "death of God." Is this just for informational purposes?

Only partly so. Increasingly when I speak, I find myself less and less interested in inserting some idea—in this case the "death of God"—into somebody's head, and more interested in reminding someone of something that may have happened to him. This is one reason we're being noticed far beyond our deserts—we have reminded people of something that has happened to them and they have decided to take notice of it too.

QUESTION 28: In radical theology, is it required that one have had a concrete experience of the loss of God? A deconversion experience, one might say?

I would hope not, for this would mean one could not come into the radical position from ordinary unbelief or secularism. But it is true that the contemporary development of what is called the radical or "death of God" theology is tied up with the breakdown of the Biblical-neo-orthodox theological position, and thus radical theology has been, in its first stages, characterized by the theme of the loss of transcendence. My answer to the question would be, I think, that the loss of transcendence is a possible way in, but it is not necessary. What is necessary is, with or without the personal experience of the "death of God," a feeling for and participation in the "death of God" as a historical-cultural event in Europe and America over the last two hundred years. That historical story must somehow become the individual's story, whatever the texture of his personal religious or irreligious life might have been. Deconversion experiences help, but do not define the radical theology.

QUESTION 29: You wrote in an article some months ago that you couldn't see any value that the radical theology might have to the church as presently constituted. Do you still feel this way?

I received a good deal of very interesting criticism when I wrote that, and largely from pastors who had become interested in the radical theology and who felt that it was possible to be committed to that theology and still live in the pastoral ministry. Early in 1966, I held a continuing education seminar at Colgate Rochester Divinity School on the radical theology, and the majority of participants were pastors. Most of them began the seminar expecting that the measure of their commitment to radical theology would be the measure of their disaffiliation from the pastorate, and they found, to their surprise and mine, that they ended our period of study with a firmer confidence that radical theology could be put to responsible work in the parish. There are, of course, plenty of problems, but I am being wisely instructed by my friends at this point, and would by no means hold to my negative words. A very high proportion of my public speaking the last three months has been to pastors and they have taught me that the situation is more fluid than I'd thought.

QUESTION 30: Is there any brief way in which you could characterize your present thinking in comparison, say, to the articles collected in your volume with Altizer? Is there any important element in your thinking now that wasn't in those articles?

Since writing the articles collected in *Radical Theology and the Death of God*, I have done a lot of refining, definition, and clarification of the main themes in the radical theology. At one important point I think there is a real difference. In some of the material in that book, *The Christian Scholar* article in particular, I talk about waiting for God, faith not as possession but hope, and so on. I wouldn't put things in this way now. There was a time when I felt it was possible to speak both about "death of God" and waiting for God, and to make use of the death-resurrection mythology to overcome some of the blatant contradictions in the two ideas. But I realized that I meant by "waiting for God" something that the phrase had no right to mean. I meant that I thought of my work as open, exploratory, incomplete. That is fine; everybody thinks of his work in this way. The point is that "waiting for God" was really too pious a description for that fact. I do not use the idea, and I handle the idea of "What do you think is going to happen to your thinking?" along the lines suggested below in the answer to question 31. In place, in a way, of "waiting for God" is the interest in the development of new approaches, godless approaches, to the sacred. (See question 16.)

QUESTION 31: How do you see the next stages developing in radical theology? What is likely to happen next?

Changes come so fast in the intellectual world today that I have found it a healthy exercise to ask myself questions like: "When the radical theology breaks down, how will it happen?" Or, "What changes in your own thought are likely over the next years?" I can answer both in part by saying that there are perhaps three possibilities for radical theology and the radical theologians:

1. They could move to the left, the way many of their Christian critics think they will move, to a candid atheism or humanism without any of the Christian claims. Perhaps Marxist, perhaps Freudian, perhaps new left— but Jesus will become as dispensible as God, and the Christian community will not be the one in which they find their comrades.

2. They could move to the right, and the birth or resurrection of God could be experienced. I cannot see how one can rule out this possibility. As far as the present theological situation in Protestantism goes, the radicals are in closest debate and discussion with two other groups, neither of them "death of God" types: with secular theology as done by Harvey Cox, and with Bishop Robinson and his explorations. This is the most exciting theological triangle I know about.

3. They could move to different items on the theological agenda. Right now, the radical theology is still in its polemic, offense-giving, publicity-oriented phase, a phase spearheaded by the phrase "death of God" and by the radicals' insistence that that is what they mean. I think it quite likely that this emphasis will fade, and that there will be less emphasis on the specific fact of God's disappearance, the mode of it, and the reasons for it, and more emphasis on the positive requirements for living as a Christian without God. Some have gods that need to die; some don't and we must not get fixated on the phrase or the event, however true. Some other items on the agenda that interest me are:

a. Christology, and the possibility of replacing the doctrine of the two natures with a historically understood *imitatio Christi* approach.

b. The doctrine of man; sin, guilt, and optimism in the radical theology.

c. The problem of the institutional embodiment ap-

propriate to the radical theology: church, sacrament, ministry.

d. The dialogue with the Jew, both believing and unbelieving, and the dialogue with Buddhism as another godless religion.

QUESTION 32: What do you say to your critics who
accuse the "death of God" theologians of
publicity-seeking, of being journalistic ex-
ploiters of a fad created by the mass
media?

I think it is too bad that the publicity could not have
come after we had done our careful, analytical work in
history, ethics, Christology, Bible. This remains to be
done; it is being done now. We did not seek publicity;
we performed a series of harmless acts, never before
known to degrade men into fad-mongering immoralists—
we wrote articles in response to a request from an editor
of *The Christian Century!* We have not sought anything,
though we have not eschewed using whatever forms of
mass communication seemed appropriate. We have written theological journalism, of course, largely upon request. I have a feeling that the wave of moral indictments
of the radical theologians is nearly over. It tended to be
made by people who had read little or nothing of the
published material. The difference between President
John Bennett's irritated note on radical theology in the
Union Seminary Bulletin last fall and his helpful article
in the Easter issue of *Look* is a straw in the wind. I'm
sure that even J. Robert Nelson of Boston University
must be a bit contrite over his quite vulgar personal
attack in *The Christian Century* last winter. (See question 24.) "Fad" is a hard word to define and respond to.
We have been picked up by all kinds of people who have
been more interested in getting a story or stirring people
up than in Christian communication. So in one obvious

sense there is an element of fad, publicity, nonevent in the whole situation. We also think that we are pointing to truth, and this makes the "fad" problem irrelevant. We would be thoroughly untrustworthy hacks if we did not think that radical theology was a possible way for men and women to think and act as Christians in our time.

THE THEOLOGIANS SPEAK FOR THEMSELVES   211

Thomas J. J. Altizer

THE SIGNIFICANCE
OF THE NEW THEOLOGY

W HAT CAN IT MEAN to speak of a
new theology? Indeed, insofar as
Christianity has existed for two millennia, how can a truly
Christian theology in any sense be new? Has not Christianity for once and for all time been given to the saints,
or finally and definitively been revealed in the Bible?
Even granting that theology may well adopt a new language, a new style, or a new imagery, must it not forever be grounded in a single and unchanging confession
of faith? These questions, common as they are, betray a
dangerous naïveté both about the discipline and practice
of theology and about the language and reality of faith.
For they assume that theological language is the sec-
ondary expression of a prior and given faith, that language itself is subordinate to and the mere passive
receptacle of an eternal meaning, and that faith transcends the actuality and the arena of its modes of expression.

The problem of the relation between language and
faith has become peculiarly acute in our time. Most
fundamentally, this problem derives from the apparent
fact that faith has increasingly become silent. As the

Previously unpublished.

historical world of Christendom has receded into a forgotten past, an established form of faith has become
unspeakable. Either its words have become empty and
archaic, or its speakers have attempted to create an
isolated and autonomous language that solipsistically
speaks only to itself, or its witness has been exercised
outside the speech of language itself. Now the Christian
God is unsayable, his name for the first time unnameable,
and those who truly try to speak in his name are inevitably drawn to the language of absence, eclipse, and
silence. No longer does the theologian attempt to speak
of faith to the world, for he is mute in face of the
contemporary challenge of faith, and is rapidly losing
the power to speak. Consequently, the root problem of
theology today is not one of speaking meaningfully or
relevantly but rather of overcoming the impediments to
the very act of speech.

If this be so, may we ask if it is necessary for the
Christian to speak? Or, at least, is it essential for the
theologian to seek an individual or new mode of speech?
That is to say, must the theologian seek a language differ-
ing from the language of the Bible, or of the creeds,
confessions, and liturgies of the church, or of earlier
forms of theology? At this point we must note that
theology, as we know it, is a unique creation of Christianity. The Greeks identified theology either with the
pure *theōria* of metaphysics or with the systematic order-
ing of an ancient and diverse body of myth. Judaism and
Islam know theology primarily as a systemization of the
sacred law of revelation and tradition and secondarily as
an apology directed to the unbeliever. Their theologies
repudiate the quest for a knowledge of God if only
because each is the product of a tradition which con-
demns all images of God. In the higher religions of the
Orient, we find neither a vision nor an understanding of
a unique and active subject of faith, and thus we find no

discourse directed to unveiling a distinctive truth of faith. Only in Christianity do we find a theology in quest of an ultimate truth deriving from the full and active presence of a self-revealing subject. Therefore, if Christian theology is to continue to be loyal to its distinctive nature, it must attempt to seek that truth which is present in the living "now" of faith.

Yet if ours is a time in which a given form of faith has either collapsed or become unspeakable, is it not far wiser for theology to exist in silence? Many theologians, perhaps the majority, have chosen a course of refusing to speak about God, contenting themselves instead with a purely practical or pastoral theology. Continually we hear urgent calls for the theologian to direct himself to the pragmatic problems of war and peace, of injustice and poverty, of mental health and illness, of the new technology and the new society. But what can the theologian as theologian say to such problems? If he cannot speak of the center or ground or goal of faith, what can he say to the pragmatic problems confronting the man of faith? Is he simply to be the popular interpreter of the scientist, the scholar, and the technician, and thus a kind of priestly journalist who mediates between the professional elite and the pious masses? No, it will be said, he is called to speak a prophetic word to the darkness and perversity of our world. He is called to seek out the foundations of the alienation and repression about and within us, and then to speak God's No to every obstacle to liberty and life. However, if the theologian can no longer speak of God, how can he possibly speak of God's judgment and salvation? Where today do we find a prophetic word of the theologian which is not a faint echo of an earlier and more powerful secular voice?

Of course, the remedy for such a situation is not a simple call for a prophetic theology. Nor can the problem be met by a repetition of the moral language of the Judeo-

Christian tradition. This language has become empty as it has been divorced from its withering religious ground, and, in any case, the children of this world have long since ceased to be interiorly affected by the language of morality. So rapid has the erosion of faith already become that even the prophetic insights of the past generation of theologians can no longer be spoken in our floodtime of unbelief. Is it not just possible then that the primary task of the theologian today continues to be quite simply theological? Theology has no greater enemies than her enemies within, and yet again today these enemies attempt to lure theology away from its fundamental task. Silence is their greatest weapon, the cultivation of a silence in which the theologian speaks only of the church, or of popular culture, or of the Christian tradition, or of those few bones which the men of power throw at those who kneel at their feet. Such silence is an artful weapon for it is almost impervious to attack. Who is to say that theology has betrayed its vocation if it speaks a judicious language of gesture and ornament which no one hears because it doesn't actually speak?

Confronted as we are by a mass culture in which there are very nearly no organs of speech, where is the theologian to seek the gift of speech? For many years our wiser theologians have refused a false language—false precisely because the established language of the Christian tradition has become empty and thus meaningless—and they have cultivated a listening which directs theology to the real questions which it meets. But in our revolutionary situation there appears to be no way to a mediation between theology and the world, apart from a radical transformation of the answers of theology or the questions of the world. The theologian who mastered the language of the artist, or the philosopher, or the scientist, or the scholar, soon discovered the very exercise of these languages numbed or dissolved all that language which he had known as the language of faith. For a time he could play at the game of speaking two discordant languages with a single tongue, with the hope that the resulting dissonance would prepare the way for the triumph of faith. Unfortunately, in this game the living language invariably triumphs over the dead. Faced with this dilemma, many theologians—particularly those who were disciples of the masters of modern theology and who could not bear to face the consequences of their master's choice—retreated from the problems of theology and gave themselves to the tasks of the church.

Perhaps the greatest obstacle thus far confronting the theologian has been his almost innate conviction that the subject of theology is given. Theology is inquiry into the acts and nature of God or it is nothing at all. True, theology can direct its study to any arena of God's acts, including the whole range of the human response of the creature to the Creator. But theology loses its ground apart from the existence and the presence of God. Almost like the naïve layman who is persuaded that the meaning of a word is determined by its origin, the theologian has seemed unable to abandon his loyalty to the theological tradition, despite his increasing awareness that the tradition itself is either dormant or moribund. Underlying this loyalty is, of course, the conviction that the Christian faith stands or falls with the eternal existence and the continuing activity of God. Thus at a time when it is no longer possible to speak meaningfully of God, theology can only preserve itself by ceasing to speak. Silence itself becomes the astute theologian's witness to faith and thence his primary activity becomes directed either to the veiling or the dissolution of all theological language. Presumably the Christian faith can now survive and triumph only when it is unheard by the world.

We cannot deny that silence can be an effective and powerful witness of faith. We can only question its validity as the sole tactic of the theologian. One irony of the modern theologian is that he has lost almost any awareness of the great religious traditions of mankind, because he has so immersed himself in a modern and all too secular world. Apparently being convinced that ultimate truth is present only in the Bible or in Christianity, he has ignored even the intense contemporary Western response to the mystical traditions of the Orient, and thus has been ignorant of the higher mystical ways of silence. This irony becomes compounded when the modern theologian seizes upon a few fragments of a Christian way of silence about God, exalting them into a contemporary way of faith for us, without any realization of the profundity and overwhelming power of the Buddhist ways of total silence. Nor do such theologians pay any attention to the primary role of silence and emptiness in modern Western literature, art, and music, or even to the meditations on silence of a Heidegger or a Wittgenstein. No, the theologian is not serious about the way of silence. His way of silence is simply an evasion and a retreat from the awesome burdens which our situation has thrust upon theology. Yet we must recognize the subtle dangers of a theological silence, and while admitting the wisdom of an occasional theological retreat, we must fully realize that Christian theology will have ceased to exist when it ceases to speak.

Language and history are the primary arenas of the contemporary theological battle, whether this struggle takes place in the context of Biblical studies, or upon the horizon of the modern consciousness and sensibility. Not that these arenas can be disjoined, for language is always the product of a particular history, just as history is meaningless apart from language. Initially, the problem arises from a rupture between a modern and profane history and an ancient and sacred language of faith. Hence the recurrent attempts to desacralize or demythologize the language of faith so as to make it meaningful and real to the profane consciousness of modern man. Theological programs of this sort are only incidentally evangelical attempts to convert the unbeliever, for their practitioners concede that the Christian today is a profane or secular man, and increasingly the claim is being made that a secular mode of human existence is the inevitable consequence of the Christian faith. Without denying this fundamental proposition, we might decry the far too easy and simple way in which it is commonly proclaimed, recognizing that theological meaning can never be achieved without a sustained and arduous struggle. For if an inherited theological language has become meaningless and unreal to the modern consciousness, including the consciousness of the modern Christian, then nothing less than a new language of faith can succeed in becoming real in a new history.

Here we touch the center of the terrible problems that plague theology today. How can theology speak if its given language has become alien, empty, and unreal? No doubt most theologians, to say nothing of the pastor or the preacher who is faced with a more immediate and agonizing responsibility, know a great deal of the deadness and the deliberation which is the effect of hollow speech. Who can blame the theologian who is tempted to retreat into silence as a result of the wounds that he has incurred by daring to speak? In our day, to speak the original words of the Bible or the established words of the church is to court a self-laceration which erodes the very powers of life and speech. Only the very holy or the very simple can speak a language that is independent of the history which they live, and while simplicity is not exactly unknown among theologians, we need not fear that their language is ever grounded in holiness. Not, of course, that the theologian or the Christian is alone today in seemingly being condemned to silence. Silence has descended upon our history, and if our artists and philosophers give witness to silence by abandoning all efforts to engage in an open or human speech, our moralists and popular wise men give their own witness to silence by employing a language that lulls both themselves and their listeners to sleep. Our Christian problem is that on the one hand we will not fully confess that our given language is unspeakable, and on the other we know as Christians that we have been given the power to speak.

Let us at once concede that both the theologian and the churchman are fully justified in being on their guard against any form of theology that will lead the Christian into a final immobility or silence, a death or exit from history. But let them confess that if the church and our established forms of theology are very nearly speechless, then our Christian situation demands a radical search for a new language and speech. By necessity, such a search will take place along avenues apart from our accepted homelands of imagery and meaning, it will move over difficult and unknown terrain, and it will require travelers who are prepared to venture into distant lands. Failures will inevitably result, and what success may be achieved will appear cryptic, exotic, and unfaithful to those who are able to retain a mooring in the Christian tradition, and perhaps will have no meaning at all to those who have lost altogether the language of faith. Yet we have only to remember that both the Bible and the history of Christianity record a long and noble series of radical ventures of faith. Nor have such ventures been absent in our century; we have only to note that the daring steps of our theological fathers have taken us to a boundary situation where each of us must either leap into darkness or stand at home and guard the shrinking island of faith.

From one point of view, it could be said that the

theological voyage to which we are called simply asks us to step into our own skins. We must awaken to our own consciousness and language by recognizing that the actual imagery and speech about us must be forged into the language of faith. Perhaps it already is to the saints among us, but it has not yet become a theological language in a full sense, although both theologians and nontheological scholars and thinkers have already employed our profane modes of discourse and understanding as the primary media for the discovery and the expression of faith. Thus far, however, there has been little theological awareness that such a usage of a radically profane language must culminate in either a dissolution or the transformation of an ancient and sacred language of faith. Faith cannot employ any language at hand without itself undergoing a metamorphosis by virtue of the new language in which it is expressed. Now that historical scholarship has taught us the revolutionary change which the exile effected in Israel, or the entrance of the church into the Hellenistic world effected in Christianity, we cannot expect that the movement of faith into our world will not have equal if not yet more sweeping results. But, it will be objected, faith already exists in our world if it is not in fact its creator. Perhaps this is true, and if so, we will have to confess that theology is not only alienated from the modern world but is even more deeply alienated from the world of faith.

There is also truth in the judgment that theology simply puts into its own language what is already present in the life of faith. Theological propositions record the confessions of faith, and when the theologian has properly done his work, the man of faith will simply say, "Of course." Whatever truth there may be in this judgment, however, must be balanced by the recognition that faith assumes a new meaning, a new life, and a new form when it is given theological expression. First, it becomes open to a new corporate, communal, and historical life. It becomes open to all, not something confined to a cult, an esoteric circle, or a private vision. Then too, it loses its interior immediacy, and while no doubt being diluted in terms of its original and intrinsic power, it becomes susceptible to being drawn into and ingrafted upon a whole new range of human needs and problems. Finally, a genuine theological appropriation of faith makes possible a new language, a new mode of understanding, and a new life, as an original act or event of faith becomes a way to the consistent expression of the totality of experience. While theology in this sense is not confined to the work of professional theologians, we may observe these phenomena occurring throughout the history of Christianity, and in their own way they even occur in Buddhism. But the point is that theology effects a transformation of faith, just as faith does of theology. Thus if a new form of faith is present in our world, it demands both a transformation of theology, and a transformation of the faith and vision underlying the new world which is dawning about and within us, if only by way of a communal and public appropriation of its new reality.

Earlier we remarked that Christian theology is unique insofar as it is in quest of an ultimate truth deriving from the full and active presence of a self-revealing Subject. Christianity both arose from and must ever continue to find its ground in the Word made flesh, the incarnate Word which has fully and finally united itself with flesh. The Christian confesses that the source of all true life and energy is in that Word, and even though the original and the dogmatically given form of the Word may appear to be silent and unreal, faith, in its Christian expression, can only exist and speak in response to the active and life-giving presence of the incarnate Word. A priestly insistence that the Word is the same yesterday, today, and forever, and must be ever known by means of its past and ecclesiastically sanctioned forms, will be closed to new and more universal or comprehensive movements of the incarnation. Therefore, a theology in search of new epiphanies of the Word should renounce a bondage to the ecclesiastical authority of the church. Instead it must open itself to the life and movement of the world and history which it confronts, allowing itself to speak the new and living languages of that world, with the conviction that true life and energy always have their origin in the Word made flesh.

Only on the basis of a living faith in the full and active presence of the incarnate Word can the Christian truly open himself to the life and power of a world and history in which God is dead. Apart from such a faith, he must either refuse our world or exist in it in silence and retreat. However, once the theologian casts off the blinders of a dogmatically established form of faith, and seeks a new and living form of faith and speech, a whole new language can become open to theology. Throughout its history, Christian theology has moved into new forms of language, but never before—unless at its beginning—has theology been called to a wholly new form of speech. Modern theology has already moved to the very threshold of such a speech, but it has halted at the boundary, and increasingly become immobilized by its bondage to its past. Above all, it is theology's refusal to abandon the God of its tradition, and to free itself from all those forms of faith rooted in the eternal existence and the ever-continuing activity of God, which has turned it away from a full movement into our world.

Is a truly new form of theology a possibility for us? This is a question which the theologian must ask himself, recognizing that a new form and a new language of theology can only evolve in response to the advent of a revolutionary form of faith. There are good reasons for believing that such a form of faith is indeed present, and present in multiple forms both before and behind us. Nor can a faith in the forward movement of the Word in history foreswear the possibility that the incarnate Word may appear and be real in forms and expressions which move beyond and even negate and transcend its previous epiphanies. The task of the theologian is not to create new forms of faith in response to the movement of the Word, but rather to appropriate the new forms of faith and vision about him in a language which will make it livable and speakable to humanity at large. Hence the theologian in this sense is a mediator between new pockets and centers of faith and the public and corporate world of the community of faith. His work is to make the life of faith fully and openly speakable in the present, whatever that present may be.

We cannot pretend that such a new form of theology has already come into existence, or that the avenues to it are established and clear, or even that the necessity of its evolution is unquestionable. But we can say that there is an increasingly large body of Christians and theologians, from almost all ecclesiastical spectrums as well as from among unchurched men of faith, who are seeking a radically new language of faith. These are not blind men crying in the dark but rather men who know that faith is present even if it is not yet nameable by a community of faith. A few theologians, following the initial lead of their elders, but being more deeply inspired by the language and vision already existing apart from theology and the church, have chosen to step forward and publicly speak of a radical theological quest. They have done so in part to convince their fellow seekers that theology can be open to a radical quest, but more deeply because of their conviction that the Christian faith must live and speak in the present if it is to survive and move forward as faith. Certainly the accomplishment thus far of these theologians has been meager.

Their work has been partial, fragmentary, elusive, and often unclear. At most it is a mere beginning, perhaps not even a genuine first step. Nor does their work fall into a common pattern or yet show signs of evolving into a theological school. But already the great response to their "fragments" would seem to indicate that theology must now pass through a new reformation, a reformation that has long been called for by many theologians but that most churchmen and theologians have resisted with all the power at their command.

It would be ludicrous to suggest that the survival of the Christian faith depends upon the success of these particular theologians or of the theological programs which they have attempted to initiate. But would it be absurd to ask if the Christian faith can survive apart from the successful establishment of a radically new theology? If not, it behooves the critics of these theologians at least to open themselves to the possibility of a new theological language, and to recognize that a new language will differ from the old. It simply will not do to expect to find the same kind of meaning and coherence, the same Biblical and ecclesiastical forms in perhaps a different kind of dress, or even the logic and syntax of previous theological modes of speech. To so identify theology with its given form is simply to foreclose the possibility of a new theology. By the same token, the honest seeker of a new theology will be in search of a new language and meaning, and will quite rightly rebel when he finds the old masquerading as the new, or discovers a language that is mere artificial posture or mimicking gesture. The fundamental question that he will ask of a new theological language is: Does it make possible or point the way to a Christian faith that is fully livable and speakable in the actual history which I live?

A grave danger falling to those who seek a new theology lies in their assessment of the actual historical world which they confront. Are we indeed living in a new history that has largely, if not wholly, broken with the old? Lines of continuity will, of course, exist between a new history and an old. But does a radical rupture or gulf exist between the historical world which lies upon our horizon and an old world which is sinking into the past? Here, this question must be theological, and it asks whether a radical new form of faith is coming into existence which alone makes possible a full or genuine life of faith in our history. If the break between new and old is not so radical, then a new language of theology can incorporate both old and new, and perhaps exist in a full and open continuity with the theology of the past. Certainly, we should welcome theological programs that seek an evolution or enlargement of the Christian tradition in such a manner as to preserve and expand its ancient form. The real question is whether such programs are now possible. A radical theological choice makes the decision that they are not, judging both that our world has broken with the old, and that a faith which cannot live in our history cannot be an authentically Christian form of faith. These judgments, I believe, unite all those who are now engaged in a radical theological quest, and if only because we are persuaded that the theological tradition has collapsed, and collapsed as a consequence of the death of the classical form of the Christian faith, we are in quest of a "death of God" theology, a theology expressing and recording a faith which can live in Christ even following, and perhaps even as a consequence of, the death of the Christian God. In this sense, a "death of God" theology is a theology that chooses to speak at a time in which God is dead. It intends to seek a theology that is truly new, a theology that dares to attempt to speak fully and openly of the Christ who can now appear and be real to us. The chief significance of the new theology, fragmentary as it is, is that it has chosen, at whatever the risk, to speak.

Gabriel Vahanian

WHAT IS MEANT
BY "THE END OF THE AGE
OF RELIGION"?

NSTEAD OF LOOKING at the world as the theater of God's glory, modern man is tempted to see the supernatural world of yesterday as the miserable theater, if not the theater of the absurd misery, of man.

Whether this modern idea of the world be true or whether it be false, it is radically opposed to the world of the Bible and of the Christian tradition. The Biblical world view is transcendental, ours is immanentist. According to Bultmann's formula, the first is mythological, the second is scientific. In the former, the "here" is meaningless apart from the "hereafter"; the contingent reality of the world presupposes the necessary reality of God. In the latter, the reality of God is no more than a hypothesis which modern science finds neither necessary nor useful; human existence has no other context than this world. Whereas the Biblical vision of the world seems shot through with religiosity, our vision frankly wants to be secular and profane. That is why modern

This article is reprinted from Professor Vahanian's book *No Other God* (George Braziller, Inc., 1966), and appeared also in the June, 1966, issue of *Concilium*. Used by permission of George Braziller, Inc.

Bible considers that God does not cease to be totally Other in relation to the world of which he is the creator, in which he yet reveals his presence. But this divine presence in the world is not mediated by his acts. The sacral concept gives primacy to nature over history. It is ahistorical, if not antihistorical, while the Bible offers us a historical and sacramental concept of the world and the human reality (Gen. 23:10–22; Ex. 4:1–17). To say that this concept is sacramental means in particular that the world in itself is not able to attest the presence of God, but can only do so charismatically, in spite of itself (Gen. 28:16 f.).

The sacral world is hostile to man. The sacramental world depends on man and offers itself to him as the theater of his activity, even while reminding him of his finitude. If, therefore, although bound to desacralize the world, early Christianity advocated a systematic refusal of the world instead of affirming it, this was, in my opinion, because the charismatic quality of the creation's sacramental power, to begin with, had not been aptly taken into account. Later, Catholicism was also to underestimate this charismatic quality of the world when it structured the meaning of the reality of the sacrament according to the categories of the sacred, while at the same time it transferred the sacred from the realm of nature to that of history and bestowed it on the social, political, and ecclesiastical institutions of the Middle Ages. As for Protestantism, if it understood holiness as belonging only to God, it did not always recognize that, because of this very holiness of God and his grace, the world had not lost its sacramental power but had been invested with it all the more significantly because it was not a right but a gift, a grace.

That is why medieval sacramentalism and Protestant spiritualism, even if they are otherwise Biblically-oriented, both represent a deviation from the Biblical understanding of the charismatic value of the sacramental world. By different paths they both seek either to make the faith a natural possibility for man, as if there were no discontinuity between the sinner and the justified man, or to make it the principle of a moral progressivism which ultimately can but lead to some sort of sociological segregationism.

Opposed to this is Bonhoeffer's thought. Accepted by so many disciples, it easily presents itself with the trumps needed to convince us. Indeed, if the sacralist tendency represents in general the surnaturalist deviation of Catholicism and the spiritualizing tendency represents the moralizing deviation of Protestantism, both nevertheless attain the same result: that of considering Christian life as based on the idea of a separation from the world rather than of an action that manifests its eschatological vocation within the world *through* the very sociocultural structures of the present world. Today more than ever the structures of the church should exist only to enable her to function within, or rather, through the structures of the world, and not vice versa.

On the other hand, the Christian's freedom justifies the responsibility he must assume toward the world. The Christian's commitment to God should be matched by a reciprocal involvement in the world. Otherwise, faith runs the risk of becoming sacral or spiritual religiosity (Col. 2:16–23), while the world is surrendered to the profane, to the *saeculum,* to secularism which is today underwriting the failure of both sacralism and spiritualism as the solution of the problem. This solution is proposed to us today as consisting in a secularized and religionless Christianity.

V

In spite of the valid and even seductive intuition of the Bonhoeffer program, it is nonetheless true that his proposal of a religionless Christianity merits as many reserves as eulogies. The drama of Bonhoeffer's thought, anchored as it is in the conviction of the insurmountable incompatibility between faith and religion, is to succeed only in substituting a new dichotomy, that of atheism and theism, for the traditional cleavage between the sacred and the profane or the religious and the secular, and in laying the foundations for an innerworldly millenarianism instead of the otherworldly and transcendental millenarianism that Christian traditionalism based on the dyad of this world and the next.

The error is to continue to consider the problem of faith under the aspect of an antinomy, that of the church and men or of God and the world, in which the roles are reversed: it is not the wretched sinner who stands before the majesty of God, but it is man in all his strength who stumbles against the weakness of God. That this means the abandonment of all claim to triumphalism, I willingly admit. I do not see the need of replacing triumphalism with a kenotic Christianity.

In like manner I willingly admit that one must render to atheism what is its due, just as to Caesar what is Caesar's, and recognize with Bonhoeffer that to try to explain God's power by man's weakness is deliberate self-deception. However, to draw the conclusion that the Christian must therefore live without God among men who are without God, as if God did not exist, amounts to shifting Anselm's *etsi Deus non daretur* from the domain of logic to the domain of faith before proffering it as the ultimate object of an act of faith. It is obvious that in the twentieth century more than ever before, humility becomes a Christian better than arrogance. But to explain the power of the "world come of age" by the powerlessness of God, when we should rather explain the attraction of atheism by the inconsistency of Christianity, is equivalent to making of God the weakness of the Christian. It is evident that Christianity should not attribute to itself any religious or cultural particularism. That we should be atheists with atheists, as Paul made himself a Jew with Jews, certainly is in accordance with the freedom which the Christian enjoys in regard to all men *for the sake of God*. This, however, is a question of human relations based on the conviction that faith can never serve as justification for any social segregation. But to define the Christian as a man whom God has abandoned and to make the world the theater of the absence of God or a domain whence God has withdrawn does not so much lead to a religionless Christianity as to the *mystique* of a faith whose axis is the dialectic of a God who is with us in the measure that we are without him.

Bonhoeffer, like Paul (I Cor. 9:19–23), wishes to make himself all things to all men. But unlike Paul who wished to do this for the sake of God, Bonhoeffer wishes to do this *in spite of God*. The distinction is not unimportant. It indicates the transposition of the problem from one level to another, from that of existence to that of a speculation about the faith, from eschatology to a *mystique* of immanentism. Bonhoeffer rejects the old sociological distinction between the believer and the unbeliever, only to pick it up again in another domain, the domain of faith where it does not belong. For faith is not composed of belief and unbelief. It merely affirms that unbelief waits in ambush for the believer inasmuch as it blinds the unbeliever. Faith is not what can separate them. Nor can it affirm itself by denying itself. The line of demarcation does not pass between believer and unbeliever; it passes between God and man. This is what Paul suggests and the Apocalypse clearly asserts: "Let the evildoer still do evil, and the filthy still be filthy, and the righteous still do right, and the holy still be holy. Behold, I am coming soon" (Rev. 22:11–12; cf. Matt. 25:31–46). He who is and who was, Emmanuel, is the God who is coming.

VI

Let us conclude with two remarks. First, if, for the Bible, the profane is just as real as the religious, the real, however, is the *eschaton*. In other words, a-religion is an eschatological reality; it is not an empirical datum of the sociological or historical order. Secondly, whether he be religious or not, man always tends toward idolatry. So true is this that he would invent God if God did not exist, or, if he did exist, man would kill the ambiguities to which existence subjects him or the ambiguities into which idolatry plunges him.

Did not Thomas Aquinas himself say this when he spoke of the imperfect knowledge which is the natural knowledge of God? Calvin also was quick to point out the source of idolatry and superstition in the idea of God that flowered from "this seed of religion sown in all men." As for Barth, while making Calvin's doctrine his own, it is Thomas Aquinas whom he approaches when he does not oppose religion to unbelief but to revelation, which he defines as the abolition and *assumptio* of religion, religion being the highest expression of unbelief. Was Feuerbach right, therefore, when he said that atheism was the secret of every religion? Or, was he wrong in not seeing that religion is the secret of all atheism?

To sum up: if it is true that the gospel could have been proclaimed thanks to a religious concept of the world to which Christianity in the end abdicated, is it not also somewhat in spite of this concept that in the time of the apostles and since then this same gospel must be thought and believed and lived? Might it not also be thanks to the human and spiritual values that atheism also contains? It is not these values that faith should fear, but the caricature of Christianity, its "simulacre," as they used to say in the past in referring to superstition and idolatry.